FROG STEPS

Small Movements Forward When the Path Isn't Clear

Dan Jayce

Bamboo Roots Publishing

Published by Bamboo Roots Publishing

Republic, Missouri

First Edition

ISBN (Paperback): 979-8-9950929-1-9

ISBN (eBook): 979-8-9950929-0-2

www.bamboorootspublishing.com

For Sayaka, Kaisei, and Sakura. Thank you for your patience and love through the process of writing this book. You are my reason for being and growing. I love you.

For everyone who's ever felt too tired to leap but found the strength to take small steps.

And for every frog I've ever moved, may you find your way to safer ground.

PAUSE

Pausing to reorient is not the same thing as being lazy.

This book does not give you permission to shrink. It gives you the right, and the responsibility, to know where you are, decide where you are going, and to move forward with purpose.

MOVE

Thinking and planning are important, but they do not produce change. Action does. When a pause is necessary, take it, then move. Hop. Three inches. Then again.

HELP

Part of becoming a better version of yourself is becoming a better person. Smile at a stranger. Pick up a piece of garbage. Be kind, just because you can. Not for credit. Not for likes. Just because you can. Even when you are tired and broken — especially then.

The People and The Frogs

This book is based on real experiences, some mine some not, and real frogs. The names of the people are fictional; the emotions, the movement, and the growth are not.

The Truth

I have little patience for the motivational guru industry. For the most part it's a multimillion-dollar industry built on catchphrases like "Go big or go home." That's bullshit. Go small, many, many times. That's how "big" is built. Every large thing you've ever admired was assembled from small, repeated actions that looked unimpressive while they were happening.

Contents

Introduction 2

Part I: When You're the Frog on the Sidewalk

Chapter 1: Moving Frogs When You Can Barely Move Yourself 7

Chapter 2: Stuck, Exposed, Vulnerable 17

Chapter 3: Freezing Is Part of the Journey 27

Chapter 4: Sometimes You Need Someone to Move You 38

Chapter 5: The Sidewalk Isn't Where You Belong 50

Part II: Learning to Hop

Chapter 6: Small Movements Matter 63

Chapter 7: Progress Isn't Linear 75

Chapter 8: Rain Makes You Move 89

Chapter 9: You Don't Need to See the Destination 98

Chapter 10: Freezing and Hopping Both Count 109

Part III: When You're the One Moving Frogs

Chapter 11: Helping Others Helps You 122

Chapter 12: You Can Be Drowning and Still Throw a Rope 132

Chapter 13: Moving Frogs Is a Practice, Not an Achievement 142

Chapter 14: Sometimes the Frog You Save Is You 152

Chapter 15: Keep Walking 162

Epilogue: Your First Walk 170

Acknowledgments 176

About the Author 177

Frogs Helping Frogs 178

INTRODUCTION: THREE YEARS AND THREE INCHES

Tuesday evening, October 2025. I'm walking the same route I've walked for three years now.

The rain stopped an hour ago. The sidewalks are still wet. The air smells like October in Missouri.

I see a frog. Small. Brown. Sitting in the center of the sidewalk under a streetlight.

I stop. Bend down. Scoop it up. Carry it to the grass. Watch it freeze, then hop twice into darkness.

Thirty seconds. Then I keep walking.

Before that night, I wouldn't have stopped. Three years ago, I was that frog — stuck, unable to move myself to safety.

That first frog I stopped for on a September night in 2022 changed everything. Not dramatically. Not instantly. But truly. Three inches at a time across three years.

This book is for the person who knows they don't belong where they are.

Not the person in free fall. Not the person who needs emergency intervention or a crisis hotline. This book is for the quieter version of stuck. The person who wakes up most mornings with a low-level awareness that something is wrong — the job, the relationship, the city, the direction — and then goes about their day anyway because they can't figure out how to change it and don't have the energy to try.

You're functional. You're managing. You might even look fine from the outside.

But you're on the sidewalk. And you know it.

This book will not fix that.

I want to be honest with you before we go any further, because I think you deserve honesty. Not a pep talk. Not a cheerleader. Honesty.

There are a lot of books that will promise to transform your life, unlock your potential, and help you become your best self in thirty days or less. This is not one of them.

What this book will do is show you how to move three inches. Then three more. Not because three inches solves the problem, but because three inches is how you start. And starting — actual, physical, imperfect starting — is the only thing that has ever gotten anyone across a sidewalk.

I learned this from frogs. Specifically, from the frogs I've been moving off Missouri sidewalks for three years on my evening walks. Small, brown, unremarkable creatures who don't ask to be helped, don't thank you when you help them, and freeze solid the moment you set them in the grass — even when the grass is exactly where they needed to be.

They taught me more about being stuck, and about moving, than anything I've read or been told.

This is what I learned from dozens of frogs and hundreds of miles of walking.

Take what's useful. Leave what isn't. And if you see a frog on a sidewalk — move it. Not because it's a metaphor. Because it's stuck and you can help.

That's the whole practice.

PART I: WHEN YOU'RE THE FROG ON THE SIDEWALK

CHAPTER 1: MOVING FROGS WHEN YOU CAN BARELY MOVE YOURSELF

The day had been too much.

Not dramatically too much, no catastrophes, no emergencies, no single thing I could point to and say "there, that's what broke me." Just the quiet accumulation of too many demands from too many directions until my shoulders felt like they were holding up something far heavier than one life should weigh.

Work had been relentless. Deadlines that kept moving closer. Projects that multiplied like rabbits. Email threads that spawned new email threads. The kind of day where you finish one thing and immediately three more appear, and you go home having worked hard for eight hours while somehow getting further behind.

I sat at my desk that afternoon, fingers hovering over the keyboard, staring at a half-finished proposal that was due yesterday. My chest felt tight, that low-grade constriction that means your body's been holding stress for so long it's forgotten how to let go.

The cursor blinked at me. Accusatory. Waiting. I typed three sentences. Deleted two.

Family needed me too. Anna was buried in college applications, essays about overcoming adversity and defining moments, the kind of prompts that make seventeen-year-olds excavate their souls for admissions committees. She'd asked me to review one three days ago. It was still sitting in my inbox, unopened, while I told myself I'd get to it "tonight" for the third night in a row.

The dog needed the vet. The house needed about twenty things fixed that I kept not fixing. My sister called about our parents, nothing urgent, just the ongoing current of worry that comes with aging parents who insist they're "fine" when they're clearly not.

And then there was the writing. The book project I'd been working on for months. The one that was supposed to be my creative outlet, my passion, the thing I did because I loved it rather than because someone was paying me. That book sat on my laptop like an accusation, barely half-finished, stubbornly refusing to come together the way it lived in my head.

Every night for two weeks, I'd opened the document. Stared at it. Written maybe three sentences. Deleted two of them. Closed the laptop feeling like a fraud. Writers write, right?

Except when they don't. Except when they sit there paralyzed by the gap between the vision and the execution, between who they want to be and who they actually are when they're tired.

By 7:00 p.m., I wasn't just done, I was defeated. The kind of done when you've worked all day and have nothing to show for it except exhaustion and a longer to-do list than you started with.

The kind where even sitting on the couch feels like a task you're failing at because you should be doing something, anything, but you don't have the energy to figure out what.

I told Anna I was going for a walk. She looked up from her laptop, because of course she was working on those essays without my help, being the competent self-sufficient human I'd somehow raised despite my own chaos. Her eyes did that thing teenagers' eyes do when they're seeing through your bullshit but love you enough not to call it out.

"You okay, Dad?"

I wanted to say yes. Wanted to be the kind of father who had his stuff together, who could handle a bad day without falling apart, who didn't need to escape his own house just to breathe.

"I will be," I said. "Just need to move."

She nodded, already turning back to her screen, trusting me to know what I needed. That trust felt heavier than it should have. Riley lifted his head from where he was napping on the couch, considering whether this walk was worth joining. He's an eighty-pound lab mix with more gray in his muzzle than I like to admit, and his consideration lasted about five seconds before he put his head back down. Smart dog. He knew I needed to be alone with this.

September 2022 in Missouri, evening after rain. The temperature had dropped into the 60s, that perfect early fall temperature that feels like relief after summer's humidity. The streets were wet and mostly empty. Streetlights reflected in puddles, creating doubled halos that made everything look slightly unreal, like I'd stepped into a photograph of my own neighborhood. I walked without direction. No destination, no route, no plan. Just movement for movement's sake. Left foot, right foot, repeat. The basic animal logic of: if sitting still is killing you, try moving.

The first frog appeared a few blocks in. Small, maybe the size of a quarter. Brown and shiny under the streetlight, sitting directly in the middle of the sidewalk like it owned the place. Or like it had frozen there, unable to figure out which direction meant safety. I stopped. The frog didn't move. Just sat there, completely exposed, utterly vulnerable. A car could come.

A bike. A jogger. Anything bigger and faster and less careful than a frog should ever have to worry about. I could have walked around it. Should have. I was exhausted. Didn't have energy for this. I had my own problems that felt insurmountable. What was I going to do, save every small creature having a bad night? But I knelt down anyway. The concrete was cold and wet through my jeans. The frog was colder in my palm, that particular cold-blooded temperature that feels alien against warm human skin. Wet. Trembling slightly, though whether that was the frog or my own hands shaking from the day, I couldn't tell. I carried it fifteen feet to the grass. Set it down as gently as I could. Watched it sit there, completely frozen, for maybe ten seconds. Then it hopped once. Twice. Then disappeared into the darkness between someone's hydrangeas.

"You're welcome," I said to the night. The frog didn't care. It was already gone, moving toward wherever frogs go after rain, probably not thinking about the human who'd just saved its life.

Probably not capable of thinking about anything except: "dark, safe, move".

I stood up and kept walking. And felt... something. Nothing dramatic, but different. Not transformed. Not like I'd had some profound spiritual experience that would change my life forever. Just slightly lighter. Like moving that tiny creature, doing one small thing that mattered, that had a visible result, had somehow reduced the weight I'd been carrying. Like for thirty seconds, I'd succeeded at something. Like I'd been useful in a way that didn't require complex explanations or perfect execution. I'd helped. Something had been in danger. Now it wasn't. That was real. That was measurable. That was done. And after a day when nothing felt done, when everything felt incomplete and failing, that tiny success hit different.

Three blocks later: Another frog. Bigger this time, maybe the size of a half-dollar. Still in the middle of the sidewalk. I moved it.

Two blocks after that: Another one.

Then another.

Some were tiny. Some were bigger. Some hopped away immediately. Some froze for so long I worried I'd traumatized them. But I moved every single one I saw. By the end of my walk, nearly four miles total, winding through my neighborhood's quiet streets, I'd moved ten frogs off sidewalks and onto grass. Ten small acts that shouldn't have mattered. Ten creatures who had no idea they'd just been saved. Ten moments of kneeling on wet concrete, cupping something small and vulnerable, carrying it somewhere safer. But something happened with each one. Some small release. Some tiny shift. Like each act of helping something smaller than me was permission to believe I wasn't as helpless as I felt. By frog number ten, I wasn't drowning anymore. I was no longer crushed by the weight of the day. I wasn't paralyzed by everything that needed doing. I was just... walking. Noticing frogs. Moving them. And somehow, that was enough.

When I got home, Anna was still at the kitchen table, laptop open, college essay abandoned in favor of her phone. Riley had moved approximately six inches, from the couch to the floor beside it.

"How was the walk?" she asked without looking up.

"Good. Moved some frogs."

Now she looked up. That particular teenage expression that's half-curiosity, half-concern about whether your parent is losing it.

"Moved some frogs?"

"There were ten of them on sidewalks. After the rain. I moved them to grass so they wouldn't get stepped on or run over."

She studied my face for a moment. I probably looked like I felt, less crushed than when I'd left, but still wrung out. Still tired. Just tired in a different way. Tired like you get after doing something that matters instead of tired from doing nothing that helps.

"You look better," she said.

"I feel better."

"Because of the frogs?"

"Because of the frogs."

She nodded like this made perfect sense. Teenagers are good at accepting weird truths without needing them to be logical. Like maybe she understood that sometimes you need to save something else before you can figure out how to save yourself.

"Want tea?" she asked.

"Yeah. I want tea."

We made tea together in comfortable silence. Her with her phone, me staring at nothing, both of us just existing in the same space without needing to explain or fix or solve anything.

Riley continued his six-inch migration, eventually settling with a dramatic sigh that suggested we were both disturbing his very important napping schedule. And somewhere in that quiet kitchen moment, tea steeping, Anna scrolling, Riley sighing, I felt something click into place. The work deadlines were still there. The book was still unfinished. The house still needed fixing.

The college essay still sat in my inbox, waiting. Life was still overwhelming. But I'd moved ten frogs. And somehow, that made the rest of it feel just slightly more possible. Not fixed. Not solved. Just... possible. Like if I could notice ten small things and help them, maybe I wasn't as broken as I thought. Maybe there was still something in me that worked. Maybe I could take small actions that mattered, even when the big actions felt impossible. Three inches. That's all those frogs moved each time they hopped. Three inches at a time, heading toward somewhere better. Maybe that was enough. Maybe that's all anyone needs to do. Maybe I could do that too.

FROG STEPS: CHAPTER 1 TAKEAWAYS

The Small Truth: When you're too tired to leap, you can still hop. When you're too overwhelmed to fix your own life, you can still help something smaller than you. Forward movement doesn't require strength, it requires willingness to take the next small step.

The Frog Wisdom: You don't have to be okay to help. You don't have to have your life together to move a frog. You can be stuck on the sidewalk yourself and still notice other stuck things. Both roles, frog and frog-mover, can be yours at the same time.

The Practice: Next time you're exhausted, overwhelmed, stuck, look for something smaller or more stuck than you. Move it. Help it. See what happens to your own sense of stuckness when you choose to notice vulnerability outside yourself.

The Question: What frogs are on your sidewalk today? Maybe not actual frogs, but small things you could help, even when you can barely help yourself. Moving them might move you.

CHAPTER 2: STUCK, EXPOSED, VULNERABLE

The thing about being a frog on a sidewalk is that you know you don't belong there.

Sidewalks are hard and bright and exposed. They're designed for feet, wheels, movement, not for small cold-blooded creatures who need darkness and moisture and the safety of places where things bigger than them aren't constantly passing by.

A frog on a sidewalk knows, on some instinctive level, that this is wrong. That it's in danger.

It knows that it should be somewhere else. But knowing you're in the wrong place and being able to get to the right place are two entirely different things. I've been stuck in wrong places more times than I can count. Literally, metaphorically, spiritually, practically: stuck in places I didn't belong, exposed in ways that left me vulnerable, frozen by fear or confusion or exhaustion while danger moved closer. The job I stayed in two years too long because I couldn't figure out how to leave. The relationship that stopped working but I couldn't untangle myself from. The city that felt wrong but I'd invested so much in being there. The creative projects that drained me instead of filling me. The commitments I said yes to that I should have declined. All sidewalks. All wrong places. All situations where I knew I didn't belong but couldn't figure out how to get where I did belong. And the knowing, God, the knowing was the worst part. Because it sat there in my chest like a stone, getting heavier every day, while I kept showing up to the wrong place and pretending it was fine.

Here's what it feels like to be stuck somewhere you don't belong:

You're paralyzed.

Stuck. Unable to move yourself to safety even though you can see the better place right there, just a few feet away. The distance isn't the problem. The problem is that moving requires energy, clarity, courage, and resources you don't currently have. It requires knowing which direction to hop. It requires believing the hop will work. It requires trusting that the grass actually is safer than the sidewalk. And when you're frozen with fear and exhaustion and confusion, all of that feels impossible. I stayed in that job two years longer than I should have. Not because I didn't know it was wrong. I knew. Every morning when my alarm went off at 6:15 and my first thought was "I can't do this again", I knew. Every Sunday night when the dread settled into my stomach like concrete, making it hard to eat dinner, I knew. Every meeting where I felt myself getting smaller, quieter, less like the person I wanted to be, I knew.

But knowing didn't create movement. Because moving required: finding a new job, updating my resume that hadn't been touched in five years, networking with people I'd lost touch with, interviewing while pretending I was confident and capable, possibly relocating Anna in the middle of high school, definitely facing the fear of failure and the unknown and the very real possibility that I'd leave this wrong place and land in another wrong place. All of which required energy I didn't have because the job was draining every ounce of energy I possessed just to survive each day.

Stuck.

Knowing you're in the wrong place but unable to access the resources needed to get to the right place. That's the sidewalk. That's what it feels like when you can see exactly where you need to be but can't figure out how to get there. You're exposed. Sidewalks offer no cover. No protection. No place to hide. You're out there, visible, vulnerable to everything passing by. Cars. Bikes. Joggers. Dogs. All of them massive compared to you. All of them moving fast. None of them necessarily looking down to see if something small is in their path. The danger isn't that they want to hurt you. The danger is that they might not even notice you before they accidentally crush you.

I remember this specific moment from that job: sitting at my desk, twenty people on the Zoom call, everyone talking about quarterly projections and market share and growth targets.

And I'm sitting there thinking, "If I just stopped showing up tomorrow, how long would it take them to notice?" Not because they were cruel. They weren't. They were just moving fast, focused on big things, and I was small. Replaceable. A number on a spreadsheet. That's how work pressure feels when you're already drowning, like you're too small to matter but still expected to carry more than you can hold. That's how family obligations feel when they multiply faster than you can handle them. How financial stress feels when it mounts higher than your ability to manage it. The universe isn't out to get you. The universe just might not notice you're there before it accidentally destroys you. And you're too tired to even shout a warning.

You're vulnerable.

Being small in the wrong place means everything is bigger than you. Everything is a potential threat. Everything moves faster, weighs more, has more power. You don't have the resources to fight. Don't have the size to matter.

Don't have the strength to protect yourself. Your only defense is freezing and hoping you're not seen. Or hopping and hoping you hop the right direction. Or both, freezing to assess danger, then hopping when the moment seems right, then freezing again because you're not sure if you moved toward safety or toward something worse.

But both strategies might fail. The freeze might not protect you. The hop might be in the wrong direction. And even if you do everything right, something bigger than you might crush you anyway through no fault of your own. That's vulnerability. Not as a philosophical concept but as a lived reality. When I was stuck in that wrong job, wrong city, wrong life, I felt vulnerable in exactly this way. Like the systems around me were so much bigger than I was. Like I didn't have the ability to fight. Like I was just trying to survive long enough to find a way out.

I'd wake up at 3 a.m. sometimes, heart pounding, running through disaster scenarios: What if I get fired? What if Anna's college fund isn't enough? What if I leave and can't find another job?

What if I'm making it all up and this is actually fine and I'm just being ungrateful?

The vulnerability wasn't abstract. It was visceral. It was lying in bed trying to slow your breathing while your brain catalogs every possible way this could go wrong. And the worst part?

Feeling like I shouldn't complain because other people had it worse. Feeling like my struggle wasn't legitimate because I had a job, had a home, had advantages so many people don't have.

But vulnerability isn't comparative. The frog on the sidewalk doesn't feel less vulnerable because somewhere there's another frog in a worse situation. The frog just knows: I'm exposed. I'm in danger. I don't belong here. I need help.

The wrongness is loud.

When you're stuck somewhere you don't belong, you don't need anyone to tell you it's wrong.

You feel it in your bones. In your instincts. In the way your body tenses and your nervous system screams "Danger" every time you walk through the door. The wrongness is visceral. It's physical. It's the tightness in your chest that doesn't go away. It's the way you check your phone obsessively during meetings, counting down the minutes until you can leave. It's how you feel smaller every day, like the wrong place is slowly shrinking you down to nothing.

I knew that job was wrong for me. I didn't need a coach or therapist or friend to point it out, though they all did, repeatedly. My body told me every single day. But here's the thing about wrongness: It's usually so loud that it drowns out the possibility of rightness. The sidewalk is so clearly, obviously wrong that you can't imagine what right would even look like. You just know: Not this. Not here. Anywhere but here. The grass exists. You can probably see it from where you're stuck. But you can't feel it. Can't imagine what it would be like to be there. Can't visualize yourself actually making it.

The wrongness is certain. The rightness is theoretical. It's like standing in that conference room, looking at my coworkers who seemed fine, who seemed to fit, and thinking: "Maybe the problem is me. Maybe I'm the one who's broken. Maybe if I just tried harder, wanted it more, adjusted better, maybe then I'd belong here too." But trying harder to belong somewhere you don't belong just makes you more tired. It doesn't make the place right. It doesn't make the sidewalk safe.

Every frog I moved that first September night in 2022 was stuck somewhere wrong. Not morally wrong. Not "they made bad choices" wrong. Just: Wrong place. Dangerous place. Place where they didn't belong and couldn't survive. But the grass existed. Just a few feet away. Safe. Dark.

Moist. Right. The distance wasn't far. The destination wasn't impossible. But from the sidewalk, it might as well have been miles away. Because when you're frozen with fear and exhaustion, when you're exposed and vulnerable and the wrongness is screaming so loud you can't think straight, even three feet feels impossible.

If you're reading this and you're stuck in a wrong place right now, stuck in the wrong job, wrong relationship, wrong city, wrong life, I want you to know: The grass exists. You can't see it from where you are. Can't imagine what it feels like. Can't believe you'll actually make it there. But it exists. And you don't belong on sidewalks. You're not meant for hard, bright, exposed places where everything bigger than you moves fast and might not see you before it crushes you.

You're not meant for places where you have to make yourself smaller every day just to survive.

You're meant for places where you can be yourself without being in constant danger. Where being small doesn't mean being vulnerable. Where you can rest without keeping one eye open for threats. The sidewalk isn't your failure. The sidewalk isn't where you're meant to be. And leaving it, even when you can't see where you're going, even when the movement feels impossible, is the bravest hop you'll ever make.

The grass is real. I promise you, the grass is real. Even when all you can see is concrete.

FROG STEPS: CHAPTER 2 TAKEAWAYS

The Small Truth: Knowing you're in the wrong place doesn't automatically create the energy to leave. Being stuck isn't a moral failing, it's a resource problem. You know you don't belong on the sidewalk, but moving to the grass requires energy, clarity, and courage you might not have while you're exposed and vulnerable.

The Frog Wisdom: The wrongness is always loud. The rightness is always theoretical until you experience it. From the sidewalk, the grass seems impossible even though it's only feet away. That's normal. That's not evidence you're broken. That's just what stuck feels like.

The Practice: Name your sidewalk. What wrong place are you currently stuck in? Not why you're stuck (that's usually shame). Just: Where is the sidewalk? Because naming it, "I'm on the wrong job sidewalk" or "I'm on the wrong relationship sidewalk", helps you see it as a location rather than an identity.

The Question: Can you trust that the grass exists even if you can't see it from where you are? Can you believe that somewhere safer, better, more right exists, even when the wrongness is so loud you can barely imagine anything else?

CHAPTER 3: FREEZING IS PART OF THE JOURNEY

Every frog I moved that first September night in 2022 did the same thing when I set it down in the grass. It froze. Not for just a second. Not a quick pause before hopping away. But a full, complete, absolute freeze that lasted anywhere from five to thirty seconds. Sometimes longer.

The frog would sit there in the grass, already in the safe place, already moved to where it needed to be, and just... not move. Perfectly still. As if the safety itself required processing. As if the journey from sidewalk to grass was so disorienting that the frog needed time to understand it had actually happened. I didn't think much about it that night. Figured it was just what frogs do. Basic biology. Survival instinct. Nothing profound. But later, when I couldn't stop thinking about those frogs, when the metaphor kept expanding in my mind like ripples in water, I realized: The freeze isn't a bug in the system. It's a feature.

We treat freezing like failure. Like weakness. Like evidence that we're not strong enough, brave enough, disciplined enough to do what needs doing. We have entire industries built around helping people "overcome" freezing. Break through it. Push past it. Force movement when everything in us wants to stop. "Just do it." "Feel the fear and do it anyway." "Stop overthinking and start acting." "Momentum cures everything." "Analysis paralysis is killing your dreams."

All of which might work for some people in some situations. But it's not how frogs cross sidewalks. And it's not how I'm learning to move through my life either.

Freezing is your nervous system processing.

When a frog freezes, it's not giving up. It's not failing. It's not being lazy or cowardly or weak.

It's assessing. "Is this place actually safe? What threats exist here? Which direction should I move next? Do I have the energy to continue? What just happened and what does it mean?" The freeze is processing time. And processing isn't optional. You can try to skip it, but your nervous system won't let you. It'll just freeze you later, at worse times, in more inconvenient ways. I froze for three months on that book project I mentioned. Opened the document almost every day. Stared at the cursor blinking at me like a accusation. Read the last paragraph I'd written.

Then closed it without adding a single word. I hated myself for it. I called it procrastination.

I called it laziness. I called it evidence that I wasn't really a writer, wasn't really serious, wasn't really capable of finishing anything meaningful. My inner critic had a field day: "Real writers write every day. Real writers push through. Real writers don't make excuses. You're just afraid.

You're just weak. You're just not good enough."

But now I understand: I wasn't procrastinating. I was processing. Processing the fear that the book wouldn't be good enough. Processing the grief that the writing wasn't as joyful as I'd hoped it would be. Processing the shame about being the kind of person who starts things with grand intentions and then watches them wither. Processing the reality that putting your real thoughts on paper means people might reject not just your work but you. All of that needed to be felt before I could write. My nervous system knew it even when I didn't. So it froze me until I was ready to actually process instead of just push through. The freeze wasn't the enemy of the work.

The freeze was the work.

The three months I spent "not writing" were actually three months of my subconscious working through everything that needed working through so that when I finally started typing again, the words came from somewhere real instead of somewhere forced.

Freezing protects you from moving too soon. Every frog I moved froze before it hopped. Every single one. Even the ones I set down in perfect grass, in complete safety, away from all visible danger, they still froze first. Because freezing isn't just about assessing current safety. It's about making sure you don't hop before you're ready. Making sure the next movement is sustainable.

Making sure you're not just reacting from fear but responding from readiness.

One frog, I remember this one specifically, was sitting on the edge of a driveway. I picked it up, carried it maybe eight feet to a flower bed that was dark and damp and perfect. Set it down gently. It froze for almost a full minute. I started to worry I'd hurt it somehow, that my hands had been too warm or too rough. Then it hopped. Not away from me. Not toward the deeper darkness. But sideways, parallel to where I'd set it down, to a spot maybe five inches away that looked identical to my eyes but apparently meant something to the frog. That's where it settled.

That's where it finally relaxed. The freeze let it figure out exactly where it needed to be. If it had hopped immediately, it might have ended up in the wrong spot, safe from the driveway but not actually right.

When I finally left that toxic job, I didn't leap immediately into something new. I froze for a bit.

Stayed in the safety of having left, but not yet moving toward what came next. People around me got nervous. Well-meaning friends and family: "You need to network! Update your resume!

Start applying! You can't just sit there! What's your plan? You're losing momentum!"

But I could sit there. And I did. Because I needed to process: What did I actually want next?

What had that job taught me about my limits? What kind of work would truly sustain me instead of drain me? What did I need in an employer, a role, a workplace? I couldn't answer those questions while I was still running from the danger. While I was still in survival mode, still pumped full of adrenaline from escaping. I needed the freeze to figure out where to hop next. The freeze protected me from hopping into another wrong place just because it was different from the last wrong place. It saved me from that panicked job-hunting energy where you'll take anything just to feel like you're moving forward, even if forward means straight into another sidewalk.

Freezing lets you feel what needs to be felt.

I don't like feeling difficult things. Let me rephrase: I don't like feeling fear, grief, shame, anger, disappointment, all the emotions that hurt when you let yourself actually feel them. I prefer to stay busy. Keep moving. Focus on the next task. Use productivity as an anesthetic for feelings I'd rather not face. For years, my coping mechanism was simple: If something hurts, work harder. If emotions surface, find a project. If vulnerability threatens, build a wall of accomplishment. It worked, sort of. Until it didn't. But bodies don't forget what minds try to ignore. And nervous systems don't let you skip the feeling part just because you'd rather not. So they freeze you. Force you to stop. Make you sit with whatever you've been running from. That three-month freeze on the book? It wasn't about the book at all. The book was just the thing I couldn't do until I felt everything underneath. I had to feel: fear that I wasn't good enough to write something that mattered; grief about paths not taken, about the writer I'd wanted to be at twenty-five versus who I was at forty-five; anger at systems that make creativity so hard when you also need to make a living; shame about being middle-aged and still figuring out who I want to be; and disappointment that this thing I loved, writing, had become another source of stress instead of joy.

Once I stopped fighting the freeze and just let myself feel those things, really feel them, sit with them, acknowledge them without trying to fix or solve or overcome them, something shifted.

I didn't magically finish the book overnight. But the freeze started to loosen. I could open the document without that crushing chest tightness. I could write imperfect paragraphs without immediately deleting them. I could make messy progress instead of no progress. The freeze wasn't blocking the work. The freeze was showing me what needed to be felt before the work could flow.

Freezing is temporary if you let it be temporary.

Here's the tricky part: Freezing is necessary, but it's not meant to be permanent. Every frog eventually hopped. Some took five seconds. Some took thirty. Some took so long I worried. But they all eventually moved. Because the freeze is a pause, not a destination. Processing time, not quitting time. A necessary part of the journey, not the end of the journey. The danger comes when we mistake the freeze for the final state. When we think: "I'm frozen, therefore I'm stuck here forever. This is just who I am now. I guess I'll never move again." That's not how frogs work. And it's not how you work either. They freeze, they process, they assess, and then they hop. Not because they've conquered fear. Not because they're suddenly confident. Not because they've figured out the perfect direction or developed unshakeable courage. They hop because the freeze is done. Because their nervous system has processed what needed processing.

Because staying frozen is no longer serving them. The processing has an endpoint. The freeze knows when it's complete.

I'm learning to trust this in my own life.

When I freeze now, when a project overwhelms me, when a decision paralyzes me, when change disorients me, I try to ask different questions:

Not: "What's wrong with me that I'm frozen?" But: "What does my nervous system need to process right now?" Not: "How do I force myself to move?" But: "What needs to be felt before I can move?" Not: "Why am I such a coward?" But: "What is this freeze protecting me from?" The answers aren't always clear. Sometimes the freeze lasts longer than I want it to. Sometimes I still judge myself for not moving faster, for not being more disciplined, for not just pushing through like everyone else seems to do. But I'm learning to trust that the freeze has purpose. That my nervous system knows something I don't. That stillness isn't failure, it's wisdom. And when the freeze ends, when I finally open that document or make that phone call or take that step I've been avoiding, it feels different than forcing would feel. It feels ready. It feels sustainable. It feels like movement that will last instead of movement that will collapse after two days.

Humans try to skip this part.

We get moved from one situation to another, by our own efforts or by help from others, and we immediately start looking for the next thing to do. The next goal. The next project. The next problem to solve. We don't pause to feel: Relief that we made it; Grief for what we left behind; Fear about what comes next; Exhaustion from the journey; Gratitude for help received; Uncertainty about whether we're actually safe now. We just... keep moving. Because movement feels like progress. Because stillness feels like falling behind. And then we wonder why we're so tired. Why nothing feels satisfying. Why every accomplishment feels hollow. Why we achieve the goal and immediately feel empty instead of fulfilled. It's because we never froze. Never let ourselves feel the journey. Never gave our nervous systems time to catch up to our circumstances. We moved our bodies but left our souls behind, still processing three sidewalks ago, wondering why we never feel like we've actually arrived anywhere.

If you're frozen right now, on a project, in a transition, facing a decision, stuck in that space between knowing what needs to happen and being able to make it happen, I want you to know:

The freeze isn't failure. It's not evidence you're weak or lazy or broken. It's your nervous system doing exactly what it's supposed to do: Processing. Assessing. Feeling. Preparing for the next movement. You don't have to fight it. You don't have to force through it. You don't have to judge yourself for it. You just have to let it be what it is: Temporary. Necessary. Part of the journey. The freeze will end when it's done. And when it does, you'll hop. Not because you muscled through the resistance. Not because you finally developed enough discipline. But because the processing is complete. Because your nervous system is ready. Because the freeze has done its work and now it's time for the hop. That's how frogs cross sidewalks. That's how you'll cross yours too.

Trust the freeze. It knows what it's doing. Even when you don't.

FROG STEPS: CHAPTER 3 TAKEAWAYS

The Small Truth: Freezing isn't failure, it's your nervous system processing. It protects you from moving too soon, forces you to feel what needs to be felt, and prepares you for the next movement. The freeze is temporary if you let it be temporary, but fighting it often extends it.

The Frog Wisdom: Every frog froze before it hopped. The freeze was part of the journey, not evidence of brokenness. They didn't apologize for freezing. They didn't force themselves to move before they were ready. They just... processed. And then hopped when the processing was complete.

The Practice: When you're frozen, ask: "What does my nervous system need to process right now?" Instead of forcing movement, create space for feeling. Journal about what you're avoiding. Sit quietly without your phone. Let yourself be still without judging the stillness. The movement will come when the processing is done.

The Question: What are you currently frozen about? And what might you need to feel before you can move? Not fix, not solve, just feel and acknowledge?

CHAPTER 4: SOMETIMES YOU NEED SOMEONE TO MOVE YOU

None of the frogs asked for help. That's the thing I keep coming back to. Every single frog I moved that first September night in 2022 was just sitting there, frozen on the sidewalk, not calling out, not waving tiny frog arms, not doing anything to attract attention or request assistance. They were just stuck. And I saw them. And I moved them. Not because they earned it. Not because they asked properly. Not because they demonstrated sufficient gratitude or humility or willingness to change. Just because they were stuck and I could help.

I'm terrible at asking for help.

I always have been. Something in my wiring or my upbringing or my personality makes me default to "I can handle this myself" even when I clearly cannot handle it myself. Pride, maybe.

Or fear of being a burden. Or that deeply ingrained belief that needing help means failing at being an adult. That competent people don't need rescue. That asking for help is admitting you're not as capable as you pretended to be. Whatever it is, it's strong. Strong enough that I'll struggle alone long past the point where struggling makes sense. Strong enough that I'll exhaust myself trying to figure things out independently when one conversation with someone who knows more than me could solve the problem in minutes. Strong enough that I once spent three hours trying to fix a leaking pipe under my kitchen sink, ruining two towels, flooding the cabinet, and nearly strangling a sink trap with my bare hands, before finally texting my neighbor Tom, who came over and fixed it in ten minutes.

"Why didn't you call me sooner?" he asked, gathering his tools. I didn't have a good answer. Just shrugged and said something about not wanting to bother him. He looked at me like I was an idiot. "Dan, I'm retired. I was literally sitting on my couch watching reruns. You think helping you is a bother?" I hate this about myself. I hate that I can intellectually understand that asking for help is smart and mature and efficient, while emotionally feeling like asking for help is admitting defeat. I hate that I encourage others to ask for help while simultaneously refusing to ask for it myself. That I can see clearly when Anna or my friends need support, but I can't extend that same clarity to my own struggles. I hate that this stupid pattern has cost me years of unnecessary suffering. But knowing I hate it doesn't make it stop.

Here's what I'm learning from the frogs:

Sometimes you can't move yourself. Not because you're weak. Not because you're not trying hard enough. Not because you lack discipline or motivation or willpower. But because the situation you're in doesn't allow for self-movement. Because you're frozen by fear or exhaustion.

Because you can't see the right direction from where you are. Because the distance is too far for your current energy level. Because you're so stuck that the act of unsticking requires leverage you don't have when you're the one who's stuck. Sometimes you need someone outside yourself to notice you're stuck and move you. Not because you failed to move yourself. But because some situations require outside intervention. Some sidewalks can't be left without a hand reaching down.

I couldn't leave that job on my own. I'd tried. For months. Maybe a year. I'd updated my resume seventeen times, each version slightly different, none of them feeling right. Started applications I never finished, would get halfway through the "tell us why you're perfect for this role" section and just... close the browser. Told myself "next month I'll really start looking". I made plans that sounded good on Sunday night and evaporated by Monday morning. Set deadlines for myself that I missed, then reset, then missed again. Not because I didn't want to leave. I desperately wanted to leave. I would lie in bed fantasizing about walking out, imagining the relief, the freedom, the possibility of doing something that didn't drain me. But I was frozen. Paralyzed by fear of the unknown. Exhausted by the current job to the point where I didn't have energy left for job-searching, the very act of leaving required energy I didn't have because staying was consuming all my energy. Stuck in a pattern that felt impossible to break. Caught in that particular hell where you know you need to change but can't access the resources to change because the thing that needs changing is the thing consuming all your resources. It was a classic sidewalk problem.

Then my friend Marcus noticed. Not because I told him. I didn't tell anyone. I kept insisting I was fine, it was fine, everything was manageable. "Yeah, work's busy, but whose isn't, right?"

Laughing it off. Deflecting. Maintaining the facade that I had my shit together. But Marcus saw.

The way exhaustion shows in faces even when you're smiling. The way a person's voice changes when they're drowning, gets flatter, loses its natural variation, and sounds like someone reading lines instead of living life. The way I'd become smaller, quieter, less like myself in the two years since I'd taken that job. He'd worked with me before, back when I was still vibrant, still had energy, still laughed easily. He knew what I looked like when I wasn't being slowly crushed. One day, after a conversation where I probably said "I'm fine" four times while my hands shook from too much coffee and not enough sleep, he said: "There's an opening at my company. Better role. Better pay. Better culture. I'm sending you the posting. Apply tonight."

Not a suggestion. Not a "have you thought about looking elsewhere?" Not a gentle "you seem stressed, maybe it's time for a change." A command. From someone who cared enough to see that I couldn't move myself.

"Marcus, I don't know—"

"Tonight, Dan. I'm serious. You apply tonight or I'm filling out the application for you."

I didn't do it alone, but I let people think I did. I say things like: "I left that job." "I made a change." "I took control of my career." "I prioritized my wellbeing." All of which is technically true but fundamentally misleading. Because what actually happened was: Marcus moved me. He saw I was stuck. Noticed I couldn't move myself. Created an opportunity. Pushed me toward it.

Wouldn't let me make excuses or defer or convince myself I'd do it "eventually." He picked me up off the sidewalk and carried me toward grass. I was the frog, frozen, vulnerable, unable to self-rescue despite desperately needing rescue. And there's no shame in that. There shouldn't be shame in that. Sometimes you're the frog. Sometimes you need a helping hand. Sometimes you need someone to move you.

The frogs didn't resist.

When I picked them up, they didn't fight. Didn't try to hop away. They didn't argue about whether they needed help or insist they could handle it themselves. They just... let themselves be helped. Trembling, maybe. Scared, probably. Uncertain whether this big warm hand was safe or another kind of danger. But they didn't fight the rescue. They surrendered to the help even though it meant being vulnerable in a whole new way, being held, being carried, being completely at the mercy of something much larger than themselves.

I'm not as wise as the frogs. When Marcus pushed me toward that job, my first instinct was resistance: "I don't need help. I'm handling it. I'll figure it out myself when I'm ready. I don't want to be a burden. What if I don't get it? What if it's not actually better? What if I fail and then you feel responsible? What if I'm making this job seem worse than it is and I'm just being dramatic?" All the ways humans resist rescue when rescue is exactly what they need. All the ways we'd rather drown alone than be saved by someone who might see how much we've been struggling.

Marcus ignored my resistance. Kept pushing. Called me the next day: "Did you apply?"

"Not yet, but…"

"Today, Dan."

Texted me that evening: "Application?"

"I'm working on it."

"That means no. You're applying right now or I'm coming over there."

He wouldn't let me stay stuck just because I was afraid of being moved. Wouldn't let me make my fear of accepting help more important than my need for help. And thank God for that. Thank God for people who care about you enough to move you even when you don't want to be moved.

Even when you fight them on it. Even when you insist you're fine while clearly falling apart. I applied that night. Got an interview. Got a second interview. Got the job. Gave notice at the toxic place three weeks later. And even then, even as I was walking out of that building for the last time, even as relief flooded through me so intensely I had to sit in my car for ten minutes just breathing, I almost didn't go through with it. I almost convinced myself to stay. Almost turned down the offer. I almost decided the discomfort I knew was safer than the possibility that awaited. Marcus didn't let me. He physically came to my house, sat at my kitchen table, and said: "You're taking this job. I'm not letting you talk yourself out of it. Sign the paperwork. Right now. I'll watch."

So I did. With him sitting there, making sure I didn't chicken out at the last possible second.

That's what being moved looks like sometimes. Not just the initial rescue but the continued intervention that makes sure you stay rescued. That doesn't let you hop back onto the sidewalk because the sidewalk feels familiar even though it's dangerous.

Being helped doesn't make you weak. It makes you lucky. Every frog I moved that night was lucky. Lucky I went for a walk at all. Lucky I was paying attention instead of lost in my own head. Lucky I cared enough to stop and help. Lucky I didn't just step over them and leave them to their fate. They didn't earn their luck. Didn't work hard enough to deserve it. Didn't have the right mindset or sufficient grit or proper attitude. They were just stuck. And I saw. And helped.

Because that's what people who care about you do. They see you stuck on sidewalks. And they move you.

Even when you don't ask.

Especially when you don't ask.

Because sometimes the people who need help most are the ones least able to request it. The ones so stuck they can't even see help as possible. The ones so frozen they can't imagine movement. The ones so exhausted that asking feels like climbing a mountain when they're already collapsed at the bottom.

Here's what I want you to know about being helped:

It doesn't make you weak. It makes you human. You don't have to earn it. You just have to need it. You don't have to ask perfectly. You just have to be seen. You don't have to prove you've tried hard enough on your own. You just have to be stuck. Sometimes, often, the help arrives before you ask for it, from hands you didn't know were reaching, moving you to safety you didn't know existed. You can fight it. You can insist you should be able to do it yourself. You can demand control over your own rescue. You can make being independent more important than being safe.

Or you can be a frog. Small. Stuck. Willing to be picked up and moved by something bigger than you. The frogs didn't have a choice, they're frogs. They can't refuse help or insist on doing it themselves. But you do have a choice. And sometimes the bravest choice isn't trying harder to move yourself. Sometimes the bravest choice is letting yourself be moved. Surrendering to the help. Trusting the hands that reach for you. Believing that people who love you see your stuckness more clearly than you do and want to help not because you're weak but because you're stuck.

I think about Marcus a lot. About how different my life would be if he hadn't noticed. If he hadn't pushed. If he'd respected my insistence that I was fine and let me stay stuck. I'd probably still be there. Still in that job. Still getting smaller. Still telling myself I'd leave eventually while the years passed and eventually never came. But he didn't let me stay stuck. He moved me. Not because I asked. Not because I deserved it more than anyone else. But because I was his friend.

And he saw me stuck. And that was enough.

There's probably a frog on a sidewalk right now, somewhere, stuck in the wrong place. Maybe it'll get lucky. Maybe someone will see it. Maybe someone will move it. Or maybe the frog will have to hop in the dark toward grass it can only hope exists, making it on its own through sheer stubborn survival. Either way, the grass is there. The right place is there. Even when you can't see it from the sidewalk. Even when you can't imagine making it on your own. Especially then.

And if you're that frog and someone reaches down to help you? Let them. Don't fight it. Don't insist you should be able to do it yourself. Don't make your pride more important than your survival. Just let them help. Be the frog. Small. Stuck. Trembling in someone's palm. But safe.

Finally safe. Because someone saw you. And didn't walk past. And cared enough to stop.

That's not weakness.

That's being seen and valued.

FROG STEPS: CHAPTER 4 TAKEAWAYS

The Small Truth: Sometimes you can't move yourself. Not because you're weak or lazy, but because the situation doesn't allow for self-movement. Being stuck isn't a moral failing, it's a circumstance. And sometimes, the only way out is through someone else's help.

The Frog Wisdom: None of the frogs asked for help. They just stayed stuck until someone noticed and moved them. They didn't resist the rescue. They didn't insist they could handle it themselves. They just... let themselves be helped. That's not weakness. That's wisdom.

The Practice: Notice who sees you. Who offers help before you ask. Who keeps pushing even when you resist. Those people are trying to move you. Let them. Say yes to the interview. Accept the referral. Take the offered hand. Being helped isn't failing, it's being seen and cared for.

The Question: Where are you currently stuck that you can't move yourself from? And who in your life might be trying to help you if you'd just let them?

CHAPTER 5: THE SIDEWALK ISN'T WHERE YOU BELONG

Every frog I moved that first September night in 2022 was in the wrong place. Not morally wrong. Not "they made bad choices" wrong. Just: Wrong place. Dangerous place. A place where a frog cannot survive long-term. The sidewalk isn't where frogs belong. Full stop. Doesn't matter how the frog got there. Doesn't matter if the frog made poor decisions or had bad luck or just hopped the wrong direction after rain. Doesn't matter if other frogs managed to avoid the sidewalk. This frog is on the sidewalk. And sidewalks are wrong for frogs. That's all that matters.

The wrongness. The danger. The fundamental mismatch between what a frog needs and what a sidewalk offers.

I spent years trying to figure out why I was in wrong places. The job that drained me: Was it because I chose wrong? Because I didn't work hard enough? Because I lacked resilience?

Should I have researched the company better? Should I have asked different questions in the interview? Was this my fault for not seeing the red flags? The relationship that stopped working:

Was it my fault? Their fault? Did I not try hard enough? Did I give up too easily? Should I have fought harder? Should I have communicated better? Was I too demanding or not demanding enough? The city that felt wrong: Should I have tried harder to make it feel right? Was I being ungrateful? Other people loved it there, what was wrong with me that I couldn't? I wanted to understand the why. I wanted to assign responsibility. I wanted to know whose fault it was that I ended up stuck in places that didn't fit. As if knowing why would change anything. As if fault would make the sidewalk safer. As if understanding how I got there would automatically create a path out.

But the frogs taught me something simpler: It doesn't matter how you got to the wrong place.

You're there. That's what matters. The sidewalk is still wrong even if you hopped there yourself.

The danger is still real even if it's technically your fault. The need to move is still urgent even if you "should have known better." None of the frogs I moved that night got a lecture first. I didn't kneel down and say: "How did you get here? What were you thinking? Don't you know better? Other frogs don't end up on sidewalks, what's wrong with you? Let's talk about the choices you made that led to this moment." I just moved them. Because the sidewalk was wrong. And wrong is wrong regardless of how you got there. Wrong doesn't become less wrong because you participated in your own stuckness. Dangerous doesn't become safe because you made mistakes.

The frog needs to move. That's all that matters. Not fault. Not blame. Not whether they earned rescue or made good choices. Just: This is wrong. This needs to change. Let me help.

The wrong place reveals itself through how it feels. You don't need someone to tell you when you're in the wrong place. Your body knows. Your nervous system knows. Your instincts know.

The wrong place feels like: Constant low-level dread that sits in your stomach from the moment you wake up; Having to force yourself through every day like you're walking through water; Exhaustion that sleep doesn't fix, that compounds day after day until you can't remember what rested feels like feeling smaller than you actually are, like the place is slowly shrinking you.

That voice in your head that keeps asking "is this it? is this what life is?" while you try to convince yourself to be grateful. The wrong place doesn't feel wrong because you're doing it wrong. It feels wrong because it IS wrong. For you. Right now. Regardless of whether it's wrong for anyone else. Other people might thrive on that sidewalk. Good for them. They're not you.

I knew that job was wrong for me within six months. My body told me every morning. The dread when my alarm went off at 6:15, not normal tiredness, but that specific dread that makes you want to call in sick even though you're not sick. But I stayed for two more years because I couldn't articulate WHY it was wrong. The pay was good. The company was reputable. Other people seemed fine there, seemed to actually enjoy it, even. On paper, it should have been great.

On paper, I should have been grateful. So, I told myself: Maybe I'm the problem. Maybe I need to adjust. Maybe I'm not resilient enough. Maybe I should be grateful. Maybe I'm too sensitive.

Maybe I'm not trying hard enough to fit in. Maybe, maybe, maybe. Always turning the wrongness inward. Always trying to fix myself to match the place instead of trusting that the place was wrong for me. But gratitude doesn't make a wrong place right, neither does resilience.

Wrong places break you down slowly.

The frogs weren't in immediate danger on those sidewalks. Not that second. Not that minute.

They might have survived there for hours. Even days if they got lucky. But they couldn't thrive there. Couldn't rest. Couldn't be themselves. Could only survive in a constant state of stress and exposure. And slowly, so slowly you might not notice it happening, that constant stress would weaken them. Make them vulnerable to things they could normally handle. Drain them until they had nothing left. That's what wrong places do.

I watched it happen to myself. Watched myself becoming quieter, more disconnected.

Stopped writing for fun because I was too exhausted. Stopped seeing friends because I didn't have energy for socializing. Stopped doing things I loved because the job consumed everything I had just to survive it. Even worse, I stopped being a present father, Anna would ask me questions and I'd realize ten minutes later I hadn't actually heard her, had just been nodding while my mind spiraled through work problems.

You don't need permission to leave.

The frogs didn't ask permission to be moved. Didn't fill out forms or make formal requests or prove they deserved rescue. They were just stuck. And I moved them. Because being in the wrong place is reason enough to leave. You don't need to prove the place is wrong. You don't need to gather evidence. Don't need to convince anyone else of the wrongness. You do not need to wait until it gets bad enough that even people who don't understand can see it.

You just need to know: This is wrong. For me. Right now.

That's enough.

That knowing, that bone-deep certainty that this isn't right even when you can't verbalize why, that's enough reason to leave.

But here's what makes this hard:

Sometimes the wrong place looks right from the outside. Sometimes other people thrive there.

Sometimes leaving feels ungrateful or weak or like you're giving up. Sometimes the wrong place is a good job with good pay and good benefits at a good company and everyone keeps saying "you're so lucky to work there" while you're dying inside. Sometimes the wrong place is a nice city or a relationship that should work or a life path that makes perfect sense on paper. And you feel crazy for wanting to leave. Feel guilty for not appreciating what you have. You feel confused because you can't articulate exactly what's wrong, you just know it's wrong, feel it in your soul, but can't explain it in a way that satisfies other people's questions.

"But what's actually wrong with it?"

"Have you tried harder to make it work?"

"Other people would kill for that opportunity."

"Are you sure you're not just going through a phase?"

"Maybe you need to adjust your attitude."

And maybe they're right. Maybe you are being dramatic. Maybe you should just be grateful.

Maybe— No.

Stop.

The wrongness is still real even when you can't explain it. The sidewalk is still dangerous even when others can't see the danger. You still need to move even when no one else understands why. Your body knows. Trust it.

The right place exists even when you can't see it.

From where I was standing, or kneeling, moving those frogs, the grass was just a few feet away. Visible. Real. Safe. But for the frog, the grass might as well have been impossible. They couldn't see it clearly from sidewalk level. They couldn't imagine what it would feel like to be there. They couldn't believe the journey was survivable.

The grass is real anyway.

The right place exists even when you're stuck in the wrong place. Even when you can't see it.

Even when you can't imagine it. Even when everyone around you insists the sidewalk is fine, you should be grateful for the sidewalk, other frogs would love to be on this particular sidewalk.

The right place is there. It exists.

Even when you can't see it from where you are. Even when you can't believe you'll ever reach it.

Even when the distance feels impossible and you're too tired to hop and you can't imagine surviving the journey. The grass exists. And you don't belong on sidewalks.

You're not meant for hard, bright, exposed places where everything bigger than you moves fast and might not see you before it crushes you.

You're not meant for places where you have to make yourself smaller every day just to survive.

Where you have to force yourself through every moment. Where you have to constantly justify your right to exist there.

You're meant for places where you can be yourself without being in constant danger. Where being small doesn't mean being vulnerable. Where you can rest. Where you can breathe.

Where you can grow instead of shrink.

The sidewalk isn't your failure. The sidewalk is just the wrong place. And leaving it, even when you can't see where you're going, is the right thing to do. Not because you have a perfect plan.

Not because you know exactly where you'll land. Not because you're strong enough or brave enough or ready enough. But because you don't belong there. And staying in places you don't belong will kill you. Maybe not today. Maybe not tomorrow. But slowly, steadily, surely.

Wrong places kill you slowly. That's their danger.

If you're reading this from a wrong place right now, wrong job, wrong city, wrong relationship, wrong life path, I want you to know:

You don't need to justify leaving. You don't need to gather more evidence. You don't need to wait until you can articulate the wrongness perfectly. Don't need to convince anyone else that it's wrong. The wrongness you feel is real. The danger is real. The need to move is real. And the grass exists. Even if you can't see it from where you are. Even when it seems impossible. Even when you're too tired to hop. Even when you don't know which direction to go.

The grass exists.

You're allowed to leave the sidewalk. You're allowed to trust your body when it tells you something's wrong. You're allowed to prioritize your survival over other people's understanding.

You're allowed to save yourself. Even when, especially when, no one else can see why you need saving. The frogs taught me that. And now I'm teaching you. You don't belong on sidewalks.

And that's reason enough to leave.

FROG STEPS: CHAPTER 5 TAKEAWAYS

The Small Truth: It doesn't matter how you got to the wrong place; you're there, and that's what matters. The wrong place reveals itself through how it feels in your body. You don't need to justify leaving or prove it's wrong. Being in the wrong place is reason enough to go.

The Frog Wisdom: The frogs didn't analyze how they ended up on sidewalks. They didn't blame themselves. Didn't try to make the sidewalk work. They just knew: Wrong place. Need to move. The knowing was enough.

The Practice: Name one place in your life that feels wrong right now. Not why it's wrong, not how you got there, just: This is a sidewalk. I don't belong here. Let the knowing be enough. You don't need more evidence than the feeling in your body.

The Question: What would change if you trusted that your feeling of wrongness is enough reason to leave? What if you don't need to convince anyone else or prove your case or wait until it gets worse?

PART II: LEARNING TO HOP

CHAPTER 6: SMALL MOVEMENTS MATTER

Three inches.

That's how far most of the frogs hopped when they finally moved. Not dramatic leaps. Not impressive distances. Not the kind of movement that would make other frogs stop and applaud.

Just three inches. Maybe four on a good hop. Sometimes only two. And yet: Those three-inch hops got them across the entire sidewalk.

We have a cultural obsession with big moves. "Go big or go home." "Shoot for the moon."

"Think bigger." "10x your goals." "Make massive strides." "Transform your life overnight." "No excuses." "Beast mode." "Crush it." The self-help industrial complex runs on the promise of dramatic change. Before-and-after photos that don't look like the same person. Success stories that sound like fairy tales. Transformation narratives that skip over the boring middle parts where nothing seems to be happening, the part where you're just showing up day after day doing small things that don't feel like they matter. We're sold the leap. The breakthrough. The quantum shift. The moment everything changes and suddenly you're living your best life and all your problems are solved and you're finally the person you always knew you could be.

But that's not how frogs cross sidewalks. And it's not how humans build lives either.

Small movements compound.

That first frog I moved, the tiny one, size of a quarter, hopped maybe three inches when I set it down in the grass. Then froze for maybe ten seconds, processing. Then hopped three more inches. Then froze again. I watched for maybe thirty seconds total. It traveled maybe two feet in that time. Two feet doesn't sound like much. It doesn't feel significant. It doesn't inspire motivational Instagram posts with sunset backgrounds and inspiring quotes in white text. But two feet was the distance from streetlight exposure to grass-edge darkness. Two feet was the difference between visible and hidden. Two feet was sidewalk to safety. Two feet built from maybe twenty three-inch hops. Each hop insignificant on its own. Each hop barely noticeable.

Each hop so small you could miss it if you blinked. But added together? Across the sidewalk.

Into safety. Toward survival.

I'm writing this book in three-inch hops. Not in inspired bursts where I write five chapters in a weekend and feel like a real writer finally, like I've figured it out, like it's all going to flow easily from here. Not at a writer's retreat where the words pour out fully formed and brilliant. Not in "I finally solved the puzzle and now it's easy" breakthroughs where suddenly I know exactly what I'm doing and every session is productive. In small, inconsistent, imperfect sessions where I write maybe three hundred words. Then stop because I'm tired or stuck or have to make dinner.

Then write another three hundred the next day. Then maybe skip two days because work was brutal and I have nothing left. Then write five hundred on Saturday morning. Then two hundred.

Then none for a week because Anna needed me and the dog got sick and life happened. Three-inch hops. Some days I look at the word count and think: This is pathetic. Real writers write thousands of words a day. Real writers have discipline. Real writers don't take this long to finish a book about frogs, for God's sake. Real writers would have finished this months ago. But then I look at the total. The compound effect of all those small sessions. Introduction: Written. Chapter one: Done. Chapter two: Complete. Chapters three, four, five: Finished. Chapter six: You're reading it right now. Thirty-five thousand words that didn't exist before I started taking three- inch hops. Not because I took massive action. Not because I had perfect discipline. Not because I'm particularly talented or fast or gifted. Because I took tiny action repeatedly. Three hundred words at a time. Sometimes less. Rarely more. But repeatedly. Imperfectly repeatedly.

Inconsistently repeatedly. Repeatedly.

Three inches doesn't look like progress while you're making it.

When you're the frog taking that three-inch hop, it feels like nothing. Feels pointless. It feels like you're barely moving at all, like you'll never get anywhere at this pace, like you should just give up because what's the point of three inches when you need to cross twelve feet? But three inches times a hundred hops gets you all the way across the sidewalk. Three inches times a thousand hops gets you somewhere you couldn't even see from where you started. The individual hop doesn't look like progress. The accumulation is the progress.

Small movements are sustainable.

The frogs couldn't have leaped the entire sidewalk distance in one jump. They're too small. The distance is too far. The energy required would be impossible for their tiny frog bodies.

But three-inch hops? Those are sustainable. Those don't require super frog strength. Those can be repeated. Again and again and again. All the way across. I used to try to change my life in massive leaps. "Starting Monday, I'm writing two hours every day. No excuses." Big pronouncement. Lots of determination. "This month, I'm completely overhauling my health.

Gym every morning, meal prep on Sundays, no sugar, no alcohol, early to bed, early to rise."

"This year, I'm transforming my career. New job, new city, new life. Everything changes now."

Big pronouncements. Dramatic commitments. The kind of goals that sound impressive when you announce them to yourself in the mirror or write them in your journal on January 1st. And I'd sustain them for... two days? A week if I was really motivated? Two weeks if I had accountability?

Then I'd crash. Burn out. Fail spectacularly. Feel ashamed. Give up entirely. Because massive leaps aren't sustainable. You can't maintain two hours of writing daily when you have a full-time job and a teenager and a house and aging parents and a life. You can't overhaul everything about your health at once when you're already exhausted from just surviving each day. You can't transform your entire career while also paying bills and managing current responsibilities and being present for the people who need you. The leap sounds heroic. The leap feels good to announce. The leap makes you feel like you're finally serious, finally committed, finally going to become the person you're meant to be. But heroic isn't sustainable. Dramatic isn't sustainable.

All-or-nothing isn't sustainable. Three inches is sustainable. Write for fifteen minutes. That's a three-inch hop. Doesn't sound impressive. It doesn't feel like enough. But you can do it even when you're tired, even when you're busy, even when you don't feel inspired. Take a ten-minute walk.

Three-inch hop. It won't transform your health overnight, but you can do it today. And tomorrow. And the day after that.

Send one networking email. Three-inch hop. It won't get you a new job today, but it's movement toward a new job. And you can repeat it. Read ten pages instead of scrolling social media. Three-inch hop. Won't make you educated or enlightened or transformed, but it's movement toward the person who reads, who learns, who engages with ideas instead of just consuming content. Do one push-up. One. That's a three-inch hop. Sounds ridiculous. Feels like it doesn't count. But it's more than zero. And tomorrow you can do one again. And next week maybe you can do two. None of these feel significant in the moment. None of them will change your life today. None of them sound impressive when someone asks what you did to improve yourself. But three inches times three hundred days gets you all the way across the sidewalk. Three inches times a thousand days gets you somewhere you couldn't even imagine from where you started.

Small movements don't require perfect conditions.

The frogs didn't wait for ideal hopping conditions. Didn't wait until the sidewalk was dry or the temperature was perfect or they felt fully energized. They hopped tired. Hopped scared. Hopped in the dark. Hopped when they barely had energy left. Hopped when they weren't sure which direction was right. Hopped when everything in their tiny frog minds was screaming to just stay frozen and wait for better conditions. They hopped anyway. Because three inches doesn't require perfect conditions. Just willingness to move a tiny bit. I can't write for two hours when I'm exhausted from work and family and life. Can't even write for one hour most days. I can't write only when I'm inspired and energized and feeling like a real writer because most days I don't feel like a real writer. But I can write for fifteen minutes. Even when I'm tired. Even when I'm not inspired. Even when I'd rather do literally anything else. Even when every word feels forced and awkward and wrong. Because fifteen minutes doesn't require perfect conditions. It doesn't require inspiration or energy or confidence or the ideal writing environment or the perfect time of day or the right mood or any of the things we tell ourselves we need before we can start. It just requires showing up. Opening the document. Typing words. Even wrong words. Even words you'll delete tomorrow. Even words that don't feel like they're moving you forward. Most of those words will feel rushed or inadequate or send the wrong message. Most of those sessions will feel unproductive. Most of those three-inch hops will seem pointless in the moment. But they compound. They add up. They get me across the sidewalk. Perfect conditions are a luxury most of us don't have most of the time. If you wait for perfect conditions, you'll wait forever. You'll still be on the sidewalk when the next rain comes. But if you move three inches in imperfect conditions? You're three inches closer than you were before. And tomorrow you can move three more inches. In equally imperfect conditions. And that's enough. That has to be enough. Because perfect isn't coming.

Small movements feel insignificant until you look back.

When I look at any individual writing session, it feels like nothing. Three hundred words? That's not even two pages. That's not a chapter. That's barely a good paragraph if I'm being honest about my first-draft quality. But when I look at the accumulated total from months of three- hundred-word sessions? That's a book. That's this book you're holding. That's over thirty thousand words that didn't exist before I started taking tiny, consistent, insignificant-feeling steps. The individual hop doesn't matter. The accumulation does. But you can't see the accumulation while you're in it. You can only see it by looking back. By turning around after six months of three-inch hops and realizing: Holy shit. I'm halfway across the sidewalk. When did that happen? It happened three inches at a time. So slowly you didn't notice. So gradually it felt like nothing was happening. So incrementally that you almost gave up a hundred times because it didn't feel like you were making progress. But you were. The whole time. You were.

Small movements matter more than big intentions.

I've had big intentions for years. Big dreams. Big goals. Big plans for transformation. Writing a book. Getting healthier. Building a different career. Creating the life I actually want instead of the life that happened while I was distracted. All of those big intentions sat in my head for years doing absolutely nothing. Taking up space. Making me feel guilty for not pursuing them. Reminding me that I was failing to become who I wanted to be. Because intentions don't move you. Hopes don't move you. Plans don't move you. Dreams don't move you. Three-inch hops move you. Actually sitting down and writing three hundred words moves you toward having a book. Actually taking a ten-minute walk moves you toward being healthier. Actually sending one networking email moves you toward a different career. The movement doesn't have to be impressive. Doesn't have to be dramatic. Doesn't have to match the size of your intentions or the scope of your dreams. It just has to be real. Actual. Today. Three inches. That's all. Three inches today. Three more tomorrow. Three more the day after that. That's how frogs cross sidewalks. That's how you'll cross yours too. Not through big intentions. Not through dramatic plans. Not through perfect execution. Through small, imperfect, repeated movements that don't feel like enough but somehow, impossibly, are.

If you're reading this and thinking "I need to make massive changes," I want you to hear this:

You don't. You need to make one tiny change. Today. Right now. Not a perfect change. Not an impressive change. Not a change that will make a good story or inspire your friends or prove you're serious. Just a three-inch hop in the general direction of where you want to be. Write one sentence. Take one step. Send one email. Read one page. Do one push-up. Move one frog.

That's enough. That's always enough. Because three inches today plus three inches tomorrow plus three inches every day for a hundred days gets you all the way across the sidewalk. Small movements compound. Small movements sustain. Small movements matter. Three inches matters. Always.

Even when it doesn't feel like it. Even when it seems pointless. Even when you're tempted to give up because surely this isn't working, surely you need to do something bigger, surely three inches isn't enough. Three inches is enough. It's always been enough. It's all you need.

Hop.

FROG STEPS: CHAPTER 6 TAKEAWAYS

The Small Truth: Three-inch hops don't feel significant while you're making them, but they compound into transformation over time. Small movements are sustainable when big leaps aren't. You don't need perfect conditions or massive motivation, just the willingness to move three inches today.

The Frog Wisdom: The frogs didn't wait for ideal conditions or perfect energy levels. They just hopped three inches. Then three more. Then three more. None of the hops felt impressive, but they got across the entire sidewalk anyway.

The Practice: Choose one three-inch hop you can take today. Not tomorrow, not when conditions are perfect, today. Fifteen minutes of the thing you've been avoiding. One email. Ten pages. One push-up. Do that. That's your practice. One three-inch hop.

The Question: What if three inches really is enough? What if the tiny, unimpressive, barely-counts action you can take today is actually the exact right movement for right now?

What would that three-inch hop be?

CHAPTER 7: PROGRESS ISN'T LINEAR

The frogs didn't hop in straight lines.

I expected them to, probably because I've been consuming too many motivational graphics about "the path to success" that show a clean arrow from start to finish. Point A to point B. Simple. Direct. Inevitable if you just stay focused.

But actual frogs don't read motivational graphics.

They hopped forward. Then sideways. Then diagonal. Then backward. Then froze for twenty seconds. Then hopped forward again but at a completely different angle than before.

From above, their path looked chaotic. Zigzagging. Random. Like they had no idea where they were going. Like they were lost, confused, making it up as they went.

But they all ended up in the grass eventually.

Every single one.

Despite the chaos. Despite the backwards hops. Despite the sideways movement and the diagonal angles and the long freezes where it seemed like they'd given up entirely.

They all made it.

Progress looks like chaos while you're making it.

I've been trying to build a writing career for five years.

If you graphed those five years, it would not be a clean upward line. It would not look like steady progress toward a clear goal.

It would look like:

Year one: Excited, writing daily, feeling inspired. This is it. This is what I'm meant to do. Started three different projects with complete confidence that at least one would be "the one."

Year two: Discouraged, writing rarely, questioning everything. Maybe I'm not actually a writer. Maybe I was deluding myself. Maybe this was just a midlife crisis hobby I convinced myself was a calling. Abandoned all three projects halfway through.

Year three: Changed direction entirely, started over on different projects because clearly the problem was choosing the wrong genre. Tried nonfiction instead of fiction. Then tried poetry. Then tried personal essays. None of it felt right but kept hopping anyway, desperate to find something that stuck.

Year four: Made some progress—actually finished a manuscript—then got stuck, couldn't figure out how to revise it, couldn't face the feedback, couldn't move forward or backward, just... frozen. Took a year-long break where I didn't write anything except grocery lists and angry journal entries about being a failure.

Year five: Finally finishing something that feels real. This book. These words. But still not sure where this is going or if it matters or if anyone will care.

From the outside, that probably looks like failure. Like I don't know what I'm doing. Like I'm not serious or disciplined or committed enough. Like I'm just wandering around aimlessly, hopping in random directions, never actually getting anywhere.

From the inside, it feels like constant course correction. Like learning what works by discovering what doesn't. Like hopping in different directions until I find the one that feels right. Like making progress even when the progress doesn't look like progress from any external measure.

Just like the frogs.

Backward isn't failure—it's information.

One of the frogs I moved hopped backward.

Not by accident. Not because it was confused or disoriented. But deliberately, intentionally backward, away from the grass I'd just set it in, back toward the sidewalk it had just escaped.

But then it hopped sideways. Then forward at an angle. Then back into the grass, but in a different spot than where I'd placed it. A spot that looked identical to my eyes but apparently meant something different to the frog.

The backward hop wasn't failure. It was the frog testing the landscape. Gathering information about which direction was actually safe versus which direction just looked safe from where it had been sitting.

Finding the right route to safety, which apparently wasn't a straight line from where I'd put it.

Sometimes you have to go backward to find the right way forward.

I "quit" writing this book three times.

By "quit," I mean: Got frustrated, closed the document, decided the whole project was stupid, walked away for weeks convinced I was done. Told myself it wasn't working, nobody would care, I was wasting my time, I should focus on something more practical.

Then came back.

Because the walking-away wasn't quitting. It was processing. It was testing other directions. It was gathering information about what this book actually needed to be versus what I initially thought it should be.

Every time I walked away, I came back with better clarity. With a different angle. With a path that felt more right than the one I'd been forcing.

The first time I quit, I'd been trying to write a traditional self-help book with a neat structure and actionable steps and a clear methodology. Came back and realized: That's not my voice. That's not what I want to say. That's not how frogs work.

The second time I quit, I'd been trying to make it inspirational and uplifting in that generic way that motivational books are supposed to be. Came back and realized: I'm not inspirational. I'm tired and messy and barely making it. That's the truth. That's what people need to hear.

The third time I quit, I'd been trying to hide myself behind the metaphor, keep it abstract and universal. Came back and realized: The power is in the specific. In my specific struggle, my specific frogs, my specific September night in Missouri.

Each time I walked away felt like failure. Like I couldn't commit. Like I was weak for not pushing through.

But each time I came back, the book was better. More real. More true. More mine.

The backward movement wasn't failure. It was course correction.

Sometimes you have to walk away to find the right way back.

Sideways counts as progress.

The frogs hopped sideways almost as often as they hopped forward.

And you know what? Sideways got them closer to safety. Not directly. Not in the most efficient route. Not in a way that would make sense on a graph.

But closer nonetheless.

Sometimes the path forward is actually sideways. Sometimes progress looks like lateral movement that doesn't feel like progress at all.

A year after I left that toxic job, I took a pottery class with Anna.

Not for career reasons. Not to build skills or network or advance any particular goal. Not because it was part of my writing journey or my personal growth plan or my path to becoming a better version of myself.

Just because it sounded fun and Anna wanted to try it and I wanted to spend time with my daughter doing something that wasn't homework or college applications or serious parent-child conversations about the future.

For three months, every Tuesday evening, we made bad pottery. Laughed at our lopsided bowls. Got covered in clay. Created nothing of value except memories and slightly-less-bad bowls by week twelve.

Anna made a mug for her best friend. It was uneven and the handle was crooked and it leaked a little from a crack she couldn't quite seal. Her friend loved it. Uses it every day, apparently. Says it's her favorite mug because Anna made it.

I made a small dish that was supposed to be for keys but ended up being for dog treats because it was the right size and Riley seemed interested in it.

Was that progress toward my writing career? Toward building the life I wanted? Toward any of my stated goals?

On paper, no. On linear progress charts, absolutely not. In productivity terms, it was a waste of three months and several hundred dollars.

But in actual lived-life terms? Yes.

That class taught me: Patience. The value of doing things badly without needing to be good at them. How to be present with my daughter without an agenda. How to find joy in processes that don't produce impressive results. How to create without the weight of it needing to matter.

All of which made me a better writer. A better human. A better version of who I'm trying to become.

The sideways movement counted. Even though it didn't look like progress toward my goals. Even though I couldn't explain to people how pottery related to writing. Even though it felt like a detour at the time.

It was progress. Just not linear progress. Just not the kind you can put on a resume or explain to someone who asks "so how's the writing going?" Sometimes progress looks like pottery. Sometimes it looks like walking dogs. Sometimes it looks like sitting on your porch doing absolutely nothing except watching clouds.

All of it counts. All of it moves you. Just not in straight lines.

Direction changes aren't giving up.

Several frogs changed direction completely mid-journey. Started hopping one way, froze, then hopped an entirely different direction.

From my perspective, this looked like they'd given up on their original plan. Like they'd lost focus or commitment. Like they couldn't stick with something long enough to see it through.

But from the frog's perspective? They just found a better route. Or the original route had an obstacle they couldn't see from the starting point, perhaps a smell of predator, maybe wrong texture of ground, maybe some frog instinct that said "not that way." Direction changes are just navigation. Just responding to information that wasn't available at the start. Just adapting to reality instead of stubbornly sticking to a plan that isn't working.

I started writing a completely different book in 2023.

Not this one. A different one. About burnout and recovery and finding your way back to yourself after you've lost yourself in work and responsibility and other people's needs.

Spent four months on it. Got twelve thousand words in. Really believed it was "the one"—the project that would finally work, finally connect, finally succeed in whatever way books succeed.

Then realized: This isn't it. This isn't what I actually want to say. This isn't my voice; it's the voice I think I'm supposed to have. These aren't my stories—they're the stories I think people want to hear.

So I stopped. Started over. Started writing about frogs instead.

Was that giving up? Was that failure? Was that proof I couldn't commit to anything?

Or was that finding the right direction by eliminating the wrong one?

I vote for the second one.

Because this book—the one you're reading right now—couldn't exist if I hadn't written those twelve thousand wrong words first. Couldn't have found this voice without testing that other voice and discovering it didn't fit. Couldn't have known what I actually wanted to say until I tried saying something else and realized it wasn't true.

The direction change wasn't failure. It was navigation.

Progress is only linear in retrospect.

Here's the trick: When you look back at the frog's journey after it's complete, you can draw a line from starting point to ending point.

"The frog went from the sidewalk to the grass." Clean. Simple. Linear. Success.

But that's not how the frog experienced it. The frog experienced chaos. Zigzags. Backward hops. Diagonal movements. Long freezes where it seemed like movement had stopped entirely. Direction changes. Doubt about whether movement was happening at all.

The frog experienced every individual hop as uncertain. As possibly wrong. As maybe not enough. As potentially pointless.

Only from the distance of completion does the path look clean.

Only after you've crossed the sidewalk can you look back and say: "Yes, that was progress. That was movement. That was the journey." While you're in it, it just looks like chaos.

When I look back at the last five years of my life, I can tell a clean story: I was in the wrong job, the wrong city, the wrong life. I recognized the wrongness. I made changes. Moved back to Missouri. Found better work. Started writing. Built the life I actually wanted.

But that's not how I lived it. I lived it as confusion, false starts, moves that felt wrong even as I was making them, decisions I regretted, months where nothing seemed to work, and long freezes where I wasn't sure I was moving at all.

The clean story only exists because I survived the messy reality.

The linear progress only shows up after the non-linear journey is complete.

But you can't wait for the clean story before you start moving. You have to move through the chaos. You have to make the zigzags. You have to hop backward sometimes and sideways often and diagonally when nothing else makes sense.

That's how frogs cross sidewalks. That's how humans cross them too.

So here's what I want you to know about your messy, chaotic, zigzagging path: It's not evidence that you're doing it wrong. It's not proof that you're failing. It's not a sign that you should have a better plan or more discipline or clearer goals.

It's just how real movement works.

Forward, backward, diagonal, freeze. Direction change, course correction, long pause, weird angle. Three inches this way, two inches that way, one inch who-knows-where.

All of it is progress. All of it is movement. All of it is part of crossing from where you don't belong to where you do.

The path doesn't have to be straight. The progress doesn't have to be clean. The movement doesn't have to make sense while it's happening. It just has to keep happening.

Keep hopping. In whatever direction feels right today. Trust the process even when the process looks like chaos.

That's how frogs cross sidewalks. That's how you'll cross yours too.

FROG STEPS: CHAPTER 7 TAKEAWAYS

The Small Truth: Progress looks chaotic while you're making it and only appears linear in retrospect. Backward hops aren't failure—they're information. Sideways movement counts. Direction changes are navigation, not giving up.

The Frog Wisdom: The frogs didn't hop in straight lines, but they all reached the grass anyway. They didn't judge their zigzags or apologize for backward hops. They just kept moving in whatever direction felt right in that moment.

The Practice: Stop judging your non-linear path. Write down three "failures" from your past that were actually course corrections. See them as navigation instead of defeat.

The Question: What would change if you trusted that your messy, zigzagging path is exactly right?

That the chaos is part of the journey, not evidence you're doing it wrong?

CHAPTER 8: RAIN MAKES YOU MOVE

Every frog I moved that night appeared because of the rain.

Frogs come out after rain. Something about the moisture, the temperature, the way wet ground feels on their skin, it calls to them. Rain brings them up from wherever frogs hide during dry weather, draws them out of the safe hidden places into the open world.

But rain also creates the problem.

Because frogs that emerge after rain don't always land in good places. They hop around in the dark, looking for whatever frogs look for—moisture, food, mates, safety—and sometimes they end up on sidewalks.

Exposed. Vulnerable. Stuck.

The rain that brought them out is the same rain that put them in danger.

The thing that made them move is the thing that made them vulnerable.

The thing that moves you often creates the problem.

I wouldn't have gone for that walk if the day hadn't been crushing me.

Wouldn't have been out there moving frogs if I hadn't needed to escape my own overwhelm.

Wouldn't have discovered this whole metaphor—wouldn't be writing this book—if everything had been fine.

If the day had been manageable. If work had been reasonable. If I'd been handling things well. If I'd felt like I was on top of my life instead of drowning in it. I would have stayed home. Stayed comfortable. Stayed in patterns that were slowly killing me but doing it so gradually I didn't notice.

The same pressure that broke me down also moved me forward.

The same exhaustion that made me feel helpless also made me notice helpless things.

The same overwhelm that put me on my own sidewalk also helped me see other creatures stuck on theirs.

The rain that brought me out is the same rain that exposed my vulnerability. And somehow, impossibly, that's part of the design.

We treat obstacles as enemies.

The entire self-help industry tells us to eliminate obstacles. Remove barriers. Optimize conditions. Create circumstances where progress is easy and resistance is minimal.

"Remove friction." "Design your environment for success." "Make it impossible to fail." All of which sounds wise and practical and empowering until you realize: The obstacles are often what create the movement.

The discomfort is what makes you leave. The rain is what makes you emerge. The pressure is what makes you hop.

Without rain, frogs stay hidden. Safe, yes. Protected, yes. But also stuck. Also not growing. Also not moving toward anything.

I stayed in that wrong job for two years.

Two years of knowing it was wrong, feeling miserable, draining my energy, becoming smaller and quieter and less like myself.

Why? Because it was comfortable. Not happy-comfortable. Not joyful-comfortable. Familiar-comfortable. Safe-comfortable. The-devil-you-know-comfortable.

I had no compelling reason to leave. Just steady, grinding, soul-draining discomfort that I'd learned to tolerate.

Humans are extraordinarily good at tolerating things we shouldn't tolerate. At adapting to circumstances that are slowly killing us. At making peace with wrong places because leaving requires facing the unknown.

I could have stayed there forever. Would have, probably. Just kept tolerating, adapting, shrinking, dying slowly enough that I didn't notice.

Until the pressure mounted. Until the rain came.

The final six months of that job were brutal.

Not gradually worse. Suddenly, dramatically worse.

Leadership changed. New management came in with new priorities and a new culture that somehow made the old toxic culture look pleasant by comparison. Projects collapsed. Teams got reorganized. Half my colleagues quit in a three-month span.

My workload doubled. Then tripled. Sixty-hour weeks became normal. I stopped sleeping well and would lie awake at 3 a.m., mind racing through all the things I hadn't done, all the ways I was failing.

Anna started asking if I was okay. Not in the teenage way. But seriously. Looking at me with genuine concern. That look that says: I'm watching you fall apart and I don't know how to help.

Riley stopped napping peacefully. Started following me around the house like he was worried I might disappear. Dogs know. They always know.

My hands started shaking from stress and too much coffee and not enough food. Lost twelve pounds in two months. Not in a good way.

But that pressure is what moved me. That rain is what brought me out. That crisis is what finally made staying more uncomfortable than leaving.

Without that final brutal period, I might still be there.

Comfort keeps you stuck.

Frogs don't emerge in perfect weather. They emerge when conditions force them to move—when rain changes the environment enough that staying hidden is no longer the best option.

Humans are the same. We change when we have to, not when we want to. We leap when staying still becomes more painful than moving.

Comfort, even miserable comfort, keeps us frozen. The job that's bad but not quite bad enough to leave. The relationship that's wrong but not quite wrong enough to end. The life that's slowly draining you but not dramatically enough to justify blowing it all up.

All sidewalks. All wrong. All situations where we know we don't belong. But we stay.

We stay until the rain comes. Until the pressure builds. Until staying becomes more painful than going.

Rain doesn't care about timing.

The frogs didn't choose when to emerge. The rain decided for them.

I would have preferred to leave that job on my own timeline. When I had another job lined up. When I'd saved more money. When conditions were better.

But life didn't care about my preferences. The rain came when it came. The pressure built when it built.

And I had to move. Not when I was ready. Not when it was convenient. When the rain forced me out.

Rain reveals what you've been avoiding.

I knew that job was wrong for me long before the final crisis. Knew within six months. Felt it in my body. Saw it in how I was changing.

But I could ignore it. Rationalize it. Tell myself it would get better. Gaslight myself into thinking maybe it wasn't that bad.

Until the rain came. Until the pressure built to the point where I couldn't ignore it anymore.

The rain didn't create the problem. The problem was already there. The rain just made it impossible to pretend the problem didn't exist.

Rain is neutral.

Rain isn't punishment. Isn't karma. Isn't the universe trying to hurt you or teach you a lesson.

Rain is just weather. Just circumstance. Just life creating conditions that force movement. It's not personal.

The frogs don't ask "why is it raining on me?" They just emerge. Because the rain makes them emerge.

We could learn from that. Could stop asking "why is this happening to me?" and start asking "where is this pressure asking me to move?"

Sometimes the rain is the mercy.

I look back at that final brutal period and I see: mercy. Not cruelty. Not punishment. Not bad luck.

Because without that pressure, I might still be there. Still comfortable enough to endure. Still waiting for someday that would never come.

The rain forced me out. Forced me to move. Forced me to hop toward something different even though I couldn't see where I'd land.

That pressure was the kindest thing that could have happened to me. Because it moved me when I couldn't move myself.

If you're in the rain right now—if pressure is building, if crisis is mounting, if everything feels like it's falling apart, I want you to consider:

Maybe the rain is bringing you out. Maybe the pressure is showing you what you've been avoiding. Maybe the crisis is creating the movement you've needed but haven't been able to generate on your own.

It's not fair. It's not fun. It's not what you would have chosen. But it might be exactly what moves you.

The rain brought you out. Now hop.

Even if you're scared. Even if you don't know where you're going. Even if every instinct says to freeze and wait for better conditions.

Let the rain move you. That's what it's for.

FROG STEPS: CHAPTER 8 TAKEAWAYS

The Small Truth: The obstacles that create discomfort often create the movement you need. Comfort keeps you stuck; pressure makes you move. The crisis that feels like punishment might actually be mercy.

The Frog Wisdom: Frogs don't emerge in perfect weather—they emerge when rain forces them out. They don't curse the rain or ask "why me?" The rain is neutral. What matters is whether you let it move you.

The Practice: Name your rain. What pressure, crisis, or discomfort is currently in your life? Stop asking "why is this happening?" Start asking "where is this asking me to move?"

The Question: What if the pressure you're experiencing isn't punishment but mercy? What if it's the only thing strong enough to move you from where you're stuck?

CHAPTER 9: YOU DON'T NEED TO SEE THE DESTINATION

The frogs hopped into darkness.

Every single one.

I'd set them down in the grass, and they'd freeze for a moment — processing, assessing — then hop away from the streetlight. Away from visibility. Away from the one source of light. Into complete darkness where I couldn't see them anymore.

From a human perspective, this seemed backwards. Counterintuitive. Maybe even stupid.

Don't you want to see where you're going? Don't you need a visible destination before you take the leap?

But the frogs didn't believe in visible destinations. They believed in movement away from danger, even if that movement was into darkness. Even if they couldn't see what awaited them there. Even if they had no guarantee it was better than the sidewalk.

They hopped toward what they couldn't see.

And every single one made it.

We've been lied to about clarity.

The entire culture of goal-setting, vision boards, and strategic planning tells us: You need to see the destination before you start moving. "Get crystal clear on your goals." "Know exactly where you're going." "You can't hit a target you can't see." "Have a five-year plan."

All of which sounds wise and practical until you realize: the frogs hit their target without seeing it.

They just hopped toward "not here" and trusted that "not here" was better than "here." Moved away from danger toward possibility. Away from wrong toward — hopefully, probably, maybe — right. Without knowing what right looked like. Without seeing the exact spot they'd land. Without any guarantee it would work out.

They hopped into darkness. And trusted.

Perfect clarity is a luxury most frogs don't have.

When you're on a sidewalk, exposed, vulnerable, with danger approaching, you don't have time to map out the perfect route. You don't have the perspective to see the whole landscape. You don't have the luxury of perfect information or a detailed plan.

You just have the immediate choice: Stay here and get crushed, or hop toward darkness and hope it's better.

The frogs choose to hop. Every time. Not because they can see where they'll end up. Not because they've calculated the odds. But because they can see that staying put is dangerous.

And that's enough.

When I finally left that job, I had no idea what came next. Marcus had lined up an interview. That's it. Not a guaranteed job. Not a clear career path. Not a five-year plan. Just an interview. A maybe. A possibility that something different existed out there in the darkness.

I sat in the parking lot twenty minutes early — because I always arrive twenty minutes early, and I almost turned around and left. Almost convinced myself I should wait until I had more clarity. That I should know exactly where I was going before I left where I was.

My hands were shaking. Not from coffee this time. From fear of the unknown. Fear of making it worse. Fear that this was a mistake and I'd regret it and everyone would say "I told you so" and I'd end up unemployed and unable to provide for Anna and — But then I thought about the frogs. Hopping into darkness. Not because they could see where they were going. But because they could see that staying put meant death.

I could only see: Staying here is killing me. This interview is a hop toward something different. Different might be better. Better is worth the risk.

That's all the clarity I had. That's all the clarity I needed.

I went to the interview.

You don't need to see the pond to hop toward the grass.

The frogs hopped into darkness trusting it was safer than exposure. And they were right. The unseen destination WAS better than the visible danger.

Sometimes the best movement is toward what you can't see, away from what you can. Sometimes you don't need to visualize success. You just need to visualize escape.

Sometimes the question isn't "where am I going?" It's "what am I leaving?"

That's enough. The leaving is enough. The hop into darkness is enough. Even without knowing where you'll land.

The next hop is all you need to see.

The frogs couldn't see three hops ahead. Couldn't see the ultimate destination or the full path. They could see the next three inches — the next possible landing spot — and they hopped toward it. Then from that new spot, the next three inches. Over and over. Never seeing more than the next hop. Never needing to.

I couldn't see this book when I started writing it. Couldn't visualize the finished product. Couldn't imagine someone actually reading these words and finding something useful in them.

I could see the next sentence. Maybe the next paragraph if I was lucky.

"It was September in Missouri."

That's all I could see. So I wrote it. Then looked for the next sentence.

"Evening, maybe 7:30 or 8:00."

Wrote that. Looked for the next one.

Sentence by sentence. Three inches at a time. No clear vision of where it was going. No certainty it would work.

And here we are, nine chapters deep. A book that exists because I didn't wait for perfect clarity before I started hopping toward it. The book revealed itself through the writing. Not before the writing. Through.

Darkness protects you while you figure things out.

The frogs hopped into darkness — away from the streetlight, away from visibility. At first that seemed like a disadvantage. But darkness made them less visible to threats. Gave them cover while they figured out where they actually needed to go. Let them make mistakes without an audience.

The darkness wasn't the enemy. The darkness was safety.

When I moved back to Missouri, I didn't announce it widely. Didn't post about it. Didn't make a production of "here's my plan and here's where I'm going."

I just moved. Quietly. In the darkness of not-fully-announced change.

Told close friends. Told family. Told the people who needed to know. But didn't open myself up to questions I couldn't answer yet: Why are you moving back? What's your plan? Isn't that kind of backwards?

Questions I couldn't answer because I didn't know yet. I was hopping into darkness. And that darkness gave me space to figure things out. Space to try different work. Space to make mistakes and correct course without justifying every adjustment.

Six months later, when I started telling more people, I had clarity. Could explain what I was doing and why. But I needed the darkness first. Needed privacy to figure out where I was actually going before anyone asked me to explain it.

Uncertainty is not the same as directionless.

The frogs didn't know where they'd end up. But they knew the direction: away from danger. Toward darkness. Toward whatever frogs need to survive.

That's not directionless. That's direction without destination. A compass without a map.

I don't know where my writing career is going. Don't know if this book will succeed. Don't know what my life looks like two years from now.

But I know the direction: Toward work that matters. Toward projects that feel right. Toward honesty even when honesty is uncomfortable.

I have a compass: Does this feel right? Does this make me more myself or less myself? Is this moving toward life or away from life?

I don't need a map. The destination will reveal itself through the journey. It always does.

You can start moving before you can see where you're going.

This is the lie that keeps people stuck: "I can't move until I know where I'm going."

But knowing where you're going requires experiencing the journey. You can't see the destination from the starting point — you're too low, too close, too stuck in the current situation to have that perspective.

You only need to see the next step.

You don't need to know where the job change leads five years from now. Just: Not here. Let's try that direction.

You don't need to know how the book ends. Just: The next sentence.

You don't need to see the grass from the sidewalk. Just: Sidewalk is wrong. Hop toward not-sidewalk.

The destination reveals itself through the journey.

Every frog ended up somewhere specific — specific grass, specific darkness, specific safety right for that frog in that moment. But they didn't know that destination when they started hopping. Couldn't see it from the sidewalk. Couldn't plan for it.

The destination revealed itself hop by hop, three inches at a time, through the act of moving.

The journey created the destination. Not the other way around.

I didn't know I was writing this book when I went for that walk. Didn't know that moving ten frogs would become a metaphor that would become a manuscript.

The book I'm writing now isn't the book I thought I'd write when I started. It's better. More true. More mine. But I couldn't have known that at the beginning. I had to hop in the dark to find it.

The destination revealed itself. Just like it always does. Just like it will for you.

But only if you hop.

If you're waiting for clarity before you move, hear this:

The clarity comes through the movement, not before it.

You don't need to see where you're going. You just need to see: Not here. Let's try that direction.

You don't need perfect vision or complete certainty or a detailed plan. You just need to know: Here is wrong. There might be something better. Let's hop and find out.

The destination will reveal itself. It always does.

But only if you hop. Into darkness. Into uncertainty. Into the unknown that might be terrible or might be exactly what you've been looking for.

Hop.

The next three inches is all you need to see. The rest will reveal itself.

I promise.

The frogs taught me that. And they've never been wrong.

FROG STEPS: CHAPTER 9 TAKEAWAYS

The Small Truth: You don't need to see the destination to start moving. Clarity comes through movement, not before it. The next hop is all you need to see — the destination reveals itself through the journey.

The Frog Wisdom: The frogs hopped into complete darkness, away from the only visible light, trusting that "away from danger" was the right direction even without seeing where they'd land. They didn't need perfect clarity. They needed willingness to move.

The Practice: Identify one area where you're waiting for perfect clarity before moving. What's your "not here" that you already know? What's your next three inches — the one small hop away from wrong, even if you can't see where you'll end up? Take that hop today.

The Question: What would change if you trusted that the destination reveals itself through the journey? What if you don't need to see where you're going to start moving toward it?

CHAPTER 10: FREEZING AND HOPPING BOTH COUNT

I watched one frog for a full minute.

It had hopped three times — maybe nine inches total — then frozen. Just sat there in the grass, completely still, for what felt like forever.

My first thought: It gave up. It's stuck again. It's failing.

My second thought: No. It's processing. It's assessing. It's doing exactly what it needs to do right now.

And sure enough: after that long freeze, it hopped again. Three inches. Then froze for maybe twenty seconds. Then hopped. Then froze.

Freeze, hop, freeze, hop. A rhythm. A pattern. Neither state was failure. Both were necessary.

That's when I understood: The freeze and the hop are partners, not opposites.

They work together. They need each other. You can't have sustainable movement without both.

We treat freezing and hopping as binary.

Either you're moving (good) or you're frozen (bad). Either you're taking action (productive) or you're stuck (failure). Either you're making progress (winning) or you're paralyzed (losing).

The entire productivity culture is built on this binary: Movement = good. Stillness = bad. Keep moving. Never stop. Momentum cures everything.

But the frogs don't see it that way. For them, freezing and hopping are both parts of the same process. Both necessary. Both progress. Both worthy.

The rhythm matters more than constant motion. And the rhythm includes both. Always. Without exception. Without apology.

Freezing prepares you for the next hop.

Every freeze served a purpose: assessing whether this new spot was actually safe, processing what just happened, recovering energy, deciding direction, letting the nervous system catch up.

None of that is failure. All of that is necessary preparation for sustainable forward movement. Without the freeze, the hop becomes reckless — likely to land you in another wrong place because you didn't pause long enough to figure out where "right" actually is.

I wrote three chapters of this book in one week. It felt amazing. It felt productive. It felt like I was finally doing it right.

Then I froze for two weeks. Didn't write a word. Opened the document multiple times, stared at it, closed it. Felt the familiar shame: There you go again. Can't maintain anything. Weak. Undisciplined. Fake.

But this time I asked a different question: What do I need to process right now?

The answer came: I needed to let those three chapters settle. Needed to metabolize what I'd written so I could see what came next.

Two weeks later, I opened the document and wrote Chapter Four in one sitting. Easily. Naturally. Because the freeze had done its work. Had let my subconscious figure out what came next while my conscious mind rested.

The freeze wasn't failure. It was preparation for the next hop.

Hopping without freezing leads to poor choices.

One frog hopped frantically. No pausing. No assessing. Just hop, hop, hop in rapid succession, like it was running from something even though nothing was chasing it.

And it hopped right back onto the sidewalk. Had to be moved again.

Because hopping without assessing means moving without awareness. Acting without processing. Forward motion without purpose. That's not progress. That's just busy-ness disguised as productivity.

I've made this mistake so many times I've lost count.

The job I left? I hopped straight into another wrong job. Six months of relief followed by the slow realization: Oh no. This is wrong too. Different wrong, but still wrong.

Because I didn't freeze long enough to process what made the first one wrong. Didn't pause long enough to figure out what I actually needed. Just hopped because hopping felt like progress. Because I was terrified that if I stopped moving, I'd never start again.

So I hopped from one sidewalk to another. Different concrete. Same exposure. Same danger.

It took six more months before I finally froze. Actually stopped. Actually let myself feel: What went wrong? What do I actually need? What does "right" feel like in my body?

That freeze, the one I'd been avoiding, the one I was terrified of, saved me. Gave me the clarity I needed to hop toward something better instead of just different. It would have saved me six months of wrong-direction hops if I'd been willing to do it earlier.

Freezing without hopping leads to permanent stuck. But the opposite is equally dangerous.

Some frogs froze for a long time. Long enough that I worried they'd never move. But they always eventually hopped. Every single one. Because freezing is meant to be temporary. Processing has an endpoint. Assessment eventually leads to action.

The freeze that never ends isn't wisdom, it's paralysis. And paralysis isn't the same as processing.

There's a difference between freezing-with-purpose and being-stuck.

Freezing-with-purpose has an endpoint. You're processing something specific, preparing for movement that will come when the processing is complete. There's a sense of "not yet" rather than "never."

Being-stuck has no endpoint. You're not processing — you're avoiding. Not preparing — you're hiding. There's a sense of "I can't" that's really "I won't."

The purposeful freeze feels uncomfortable but generative. Like something is working itself out even though you can't see it yet. Like the stillness has purpose even when you can't articulate what that purpose is.

Being stuck feels heavy. Immovable. Dead. Like you're choosing paralysis because movement is too scary, and calling that choice "processing" to make yourself feel better about not moving.

The purposeful freeze eventually ends. Being stuck continues until something external breaks you out of it — usually the kind of crisis we talked about in Chapter 8. The rain that forces you to move when you won't move yourself.

The rhythm is responsive, not rigid.

The frogs didn't freeze on a schedule. Didn't hop at predetermined intervals. They responded to what they encountered. Froze when they needed assessment. Hopped when the way felt clear. Let the rhythm emerge from the situation rather than imposing a rhythm on it.

Every frog had its own rhythm based on what it needed in that moment, with that particular nervous system. There was no "right" rhythm. Just each frog's rhythm.

I used to try to impose rhythms on my writing. "Thirty minutes on, ten off, repeat three times every morning." Rigid. Scheduled. The kind of routine that sounds disciplined and like what "real writers" do.

It never worked. Not once. Because some days I needed to write for two hours without stopping. Some days I needed to freeze after fifteen minutes because I'd hit something that needed processing. Forcing a break on good days felt violent. Forcing a session on bad days just created garbage I'd delete later.

Now I try to be more responsive. Write when writing wants to happen. Freeze when the freeze feels necessary. Trust the rhythm that emerges rather than forcing the rhythm I think should exist.

Some days that means no writing. Some days it means chapters. Some days it means sitting with the document open for an hour, not typing, just thinking. Some days it means three hours straight and forgetting to eat.

All of it is progress. All of it is the work. The right rhythm is whatever rhythm actually works for my nervous system on this particular day, not what works for other writers, not what productivity experts recommend. Whatever rhythm lets me keep showing up. Keep moving forward even when forward looks like stillness.

The goal isn't constant motion — it's sustainable rhythm.

Constant hopping exhausts you. Leads to poor choices. Burns you out. Gets you back onto sidewalks you worked hard to leave.

Constant freezing paralyzes you. Keeps you stuck. Lets danger get closer while you sit immobile.

But freeze-hop-freeze-hop? That rhythm crosses sidewalks. That rhythm sustains. Because you're not burning yourself out or paralyzing yourself — you're moving the way bodies are intended move. The way nervous systems are designed work. The way humans actually function when we stop trying to be machines.

Frogs need rest and action. Stillness and movement. Freezing and hopping. Both. Always both.

That's the rhythm that works. Not just for frogs. For all of us.

If you're frozen right now, that's okay. Maybe you're processing. Maybe you're recovering. Maybe your nervous system knows something you don't and is keeping you still until it's actually safe to move.

Freeze isn't failure. Unless it never ends. Unless you're stuck instead of processing. Unless you're avoiding instead of preparing.

If you're hopping frantically right now, that's okay too. Hopping isn't wrong. Unless you never pause to assess whether you're hopping toward something better or just hopping because hopping feels like progress. Unless the momentum is carrying you away from yourself instead of toward yourself.

The rhythm you need might not match anyone else's rhythm.

Some frogs froze for five seconds. Some froze for thirty. Both made it. Some hopped rapidly. Some hopped slowly. Every frog's rhythm worked for that frog.

Your rhythm might look nothing like the person you admire, the productivity expert you follow, the writer whose process you read about. It might be freeze-long—hop-short, or hop-hop-hop—then-freeze, or something that changes daily and has no discernible pattern.

The frogs don't explain their rhythm. Don't justify it. Don't apologize for freezing too long or hopping too quickly. They just live it. And it works.

Yours will too. If you let it be what it actually is instead of what you think it should be.

Both states are progress.

When you're frozen, you're not failing. You're processing, assessing, recovering, preparing. That's work. That counts.

When you're hopping, you're not just performing. You're moving, testing, discovering, advancing. That's work. That counts.

Both serve the journey. Both are necessary. The frog that's frozen is making progress just as much as the frog that's hopping. Just different progress. Just a different phase of the same crossing.

Freeze when you need to freeze. Hop when you need to hop. Trust the rhythm that emerges. Let both states be enough.

That's how frogs survive. That's how you'll make it too.

Freeze and hop. Stillness and movement. Rest and action.

Both. Always both.

Trust it.

FROG STEPS: CHAPTER 10 TAKEAWAYS

The Small Truth: Freezing and hopping aren't opposites — they're partners. Both are necessary. Both are progress. Hopping without freezing leads to poor choices. Freezing without hopping leads to permanent stuck. The rhythm matters more than constant motion.

The Frog Wisdom: Frogs that successfully cross sidewalks do both: freeze to assess, hop to move, freeze to reassess, hop again. The rhythm is responsive, not rigid. They don't apologize for freezing too long or hopping too quickly. They trust the process of alternation.

The Practice: Notice your current state. Are you frozen or hopping? Have you been in this state too long? If frozen too long, take one small hop even without perfect clarity. If hopping desperately, freeze deliberately — give yourself permission to pause, assess, recover before the next move.

The Question: What would change if you stopped judging the freezes as failure and started seeing them as necessary parts of your rhythm? What if both freezing and hopping count equally as progress?

PART III: WHEN YOU'RE THE ONE MOVING FROGS

CHAPTER 11: HELPING OTHERS HELPS YOU

I didn't go for that walk to help frogs.

I went for a walk because I was drowning. Because work was too much and writing wasn't working and family needed more than I had and I needed to move my body before I exploded or imploded or just stopped functioning entirely.

The frogs were incidental. A distraction. Something small that happened to be there while I was trying to survive my own crisis.

But here's what I didn't expect: every time I stopped to move a frog, I felt lighter.

Not metaphorically. Not in some vague spiritual sense. Actually, physically lighter. Like each small act of helping something smaller than me reduced the weight I was carrying.

By the tenth frog, I wasn't drowning anymore.

Not because my problems had solved themselves. The work deadlines were still there. The unfinished book was still on my laptop. Anna's college essays still needed review. Life was still overwhelming.

But I'd spent over an hour noticing things smaller and more vulnerable than me, and doing something — however small, to help. That changed something fundamental. Not in my circumstances. In me.

Here's the paradox I discovered that first September night:

Helping others when you can barely help yourself doesn't deplete you. It restores you.

Which makes no logical sense. Which defies every message about self-care and putting your own oxygen mask on first. But it's true anyway. And I've tested it hundreds of times since. It works every single time.

When I'm drowning and I stop to help someone else stay afloat — I feel less like I'm drowning. When I'm empty and I give what little I have left — I feel less empty. When I'm stuck and I help someone else get unstuck — I feel less stuck.

It shouldn't work. But it does.

Helping shifts your perspective.

When you're drowning, your world narrows. Everything becomes about your own survival. Your own problems fill your entire field of vision, block out everything else, become the whole universe.

But then you notice something smaller than you. More vulnerable. More stuck. More in need.

And suddenly, for just a moment, your perspective shifts. Your problems don't disappear — but they shift from "the entire universe of existence" to "one part of a larger world where other beings are also struggling." That shift from "only me" to "not just me" creates breathing room. Creates the possibility of movement.

I was convinced I had nothing left to give that September evening. Empty. Running on fumes. If someone had asked me for help, I would have said: I can't. I have nothing left.

And then I saw a tiny creature even more helpless than I felt. And I had enough to move it. Just barely enough. But enough.

Enough to kneel down. Enough to pick it up. Enough to carry it fifteen feet.

I wasn't as empty as I thought.

In moving it, I discovered: I still had capacity — small capacity, but real capacity — to help. That discovery changed everything. Not because moving frogs solved my work problems or fixed my exhaustion. But because it reminded me: Even in depletion, I still have something to give. Which means I'm not as empty as I feel.

And if I'm not as empty as I feel, maybe I can survive this.

Helping gives you a win when everything else feels like losing.

I'd spent all day failing. Failing to meet deadlines. Failing to write. Failing to be the parent I wanted to be — Anna's essay had been sitting unopened in my inbox for three days. Failing at basic adult responsibilities. Every single thing felt like failure.

And then I moved a frog. And that tiny creature hopped away to safety. And I succeeded at something.

The smallest possible something. Moving a creature the size of a quarter fifteen feet to the left. But something.

It broke the losing streak. It interrupted the narrative of I can't do anything right. It proved: I can still make things better, even if the things are very small and the better is only slightly better.

When you're drowning in failure, even the smallest success feels like salvation.

Helping connects you to something beyond your own suffering.

When you're drowning, you're alone. Isolated in your own struggle. Trapped inside your own head. And the isolation is sometimes worse than the actual problems, the feeling that no one else struggles like this, that you're the only one who can't keep their shit together while everyone else seems fine.

Helping, even helping a frog, reconnects you to the reality that other beings are also vulnerable and struggling, to your own capacity to show up for something beyond yourself, and to the truth that you're not the only one who needs to be rescued.

That connection doesn't fix your problems. But it breaks the isolation. Reminds you that you're part of something larger than your own suffering. And somehow, that helps.

Helping creates immediate meaning when everything feels meaningless.

On days when work feels pointless and progress feels impossible and nothing you do seems to matter — helping creates instant, visible meaning.

You see a frog on a sidewalk. You move it. It hops away. It's safer now than it was thirty seconds ago.

That matters. Visibly. Immediately. Undeniably. You created positive change, right now, with your own hands. No ambiguity. No waiting to see if it made a difference.

And when your entire week feels like it doesn't matter, like nothing you do makes any real difference — that moment of clear, immediate, visible meaning is medicine. Proof that your actions still have impact. That you still matter.

Even if the only thing you did today was move something small fifteen feet to the left.

That's enough.

Helping shifts your perspective from "everything is impossible" to "this one thing is possible." It reminds you that you're not empty — you still have something to give. It gives you wins when everything else feels like losing. It connects you beyond your own suffering and breaks the isolation. It creates immediate, visible meaning when everything feels meaningless.

All of that from moving frogs. From doing the smallest possible thing for creatures smaller than you.

Imagine what happens when you help people. When you notice human vulnerability and respond to it.

You're not being selfless. You're not being noble. You're being saved. By the very act of helping.

That's the paradox. That's the secret the frogs taught me.

Helping others helps you. Not in some vague karmic sense. Not eventually, someday, if you're lucky. Immediately. Tangibly. Right now. As you help.

The act of noticing someone else's struggle and responding to it — that's what shifts something in you.

Three years later, I still do this.

Anna mentioned she was stressed about an upcoming exam last week. I was drowning in my own deadlines, definitely didn't have time to help with anything. I spent twenty minutes helping her make flashcards anyway. And at the end of those twenty minutes, I felt less overwhelmed. Not because my deadlines disappeared. But because I'd succeeded at something, which reminded me I wasn't completely useless even when everything else felt like failure.

My neighbor Tom needed someone to sit with his wife for an hour while he ran errands. She has dementia, can't be left alone. I had a book to finish. No time for anything extra. I sat with her anyway. Listened to her tell me stories I'd heard before. Held her hand. Made her tea.

When I came home and opened my laptop, the words flowed easier. Not because sitting with her solved my writing problems. But because helping reminded me why I write in the first place — to help people feel less alone. And I can't do that if I'm so consumed by my own isolation that I can't see anyone else's.

This isn't theory. This is tested practice. Three years of proof.

When I'm drowning and I help someone else, I drown less. Every single time.

So here's my invitation:

When you're drowning, find a frog. Something small you can help even in your depleted state. Something smaller or more vulnerable or more stuck than you feel.

And help it.

Not because you should. Not because it's noble. But because helping will help you. Because noticing something else's need will shift your perspective. Because succeeding at one small thing will break your losing streak. Because creating immediate visible meaning will remind you that your actions still matter.

Move it. Notice what happens in you. Not in grand philosophical terms — but immediately: Do you feel slightly lighter? Slightly more useful? Slightly less trapped in your own head?

That's the restoration that comes through helping. That's the paradox the frogs taught me.

You don't have to believe it. You don't have to understand it. You just have to try it.

Find a frog. Move it. See what happens.

Something will shift. Not everything. Not dramatically. Not permanently. But enough. Just enough to keep going.

That's all you need.

FROG STEPS: CHAPTER 11 TAKEAWAYS

The Small Truth: Helping others when you can barely help yourself doesn't deplete you — it restores you. It shifts perspective, reminds you you're not empty, gives you wins, connects you beyond your suffering, and creates immediate meaning when everything feels meaningless.

The Frog Wisdom: The frogs didn't cure my problems. They gave me something else: the experience of being useful. Of making a difference. Of succeeding at something small when everything else felt like failure. That shift from drowning to breathing came through helping, not through solving my own problems first.

The Practice: When you're drowning, find a frog. Something small you can help even in your depleted state. Move it. Notice what happens in you — not philosophically, but immediately. Do you feel slightly lighter? Slightly less trapped? That's the restoration that comes through helping.

The Question: What small thing could you help today, even though you can barely help yourself? Not a big commitment. Not a major sacrifice. Just a frog. Who or what is your frog?

CHAPTER 12: YOU CAN BE DROWNING AND STILL THROW A ROPE

The frogs I moved were stuck. Vulnerable. In danger.

I was also stuck. Also vulnerable. Also in danger of a different kind.

Both things were true at the same time.

I didn't need to be unstuck before I could help them get unstuck. Didn't need to be safe before I could move them to safety. Didn't need to be okay before I could help them be okay.

I was the frog on the sidewalk. And I was the person moving frogs. Both. Simultaneously. Without contradiction.

We have this idea that helping requires strength.

That you have to be healthy before you can help the sick. Stable before you can help the unstable. Fixed before you can help fix. That helping is something strong people do for weak people — and if you're struggling, you're disqualified until you stop struggling.

But that's not how it works in real life. In real life, you're often both. Drowning and throwing ropes. Struggling and supporting. Barely keeping your head above water while still reaching for someone else who's sinking.

Being the frog and the frog-mover. At the exact same time.

I was barely functional that September evening. Exhausted beyond exhausted. Overwhelmed to the point of breakdown. My jaw tight from stress. My chest tight from anxiety. My mind still racing through all the ways I was failing.

I was a frog on a sidewalk. Exposed. Vulnerable. Stuck.

And I still stopped to help other frogs. Not because I'd solved my own problems first. Not because I'd reached some elevated place where I had capacity to spare. But because they were there. And stuck. And I could help even though I was also stuck.

My stuckness didn't prevent me from helping. My drowning didn't stop me from throwing ropes. I was both. At the same time. Always.

Your brokenness doesn't disqualify you from helping.

You don't have to be fixed to help fix things. You don't have to be healed to help heal. Your mess doesn't disqualify you — if anything, it qualifies you. Because you know what stuck feels like. You know what it's like to need help and not know if help will come.

That knowing — that intimate, visceral understanding of struggle — makes you better at helping, not worse.

You see frogs on sidewalks because you've been a frog on a sidewalk. You notice vulnerability because you're vulnerable. The helpers who've never been helped don't see as clearly. The rescuers who've never needed rescue don't understand as deeply.

But you? You see. Because you've been there. Because you are there. Right now. Still.

The frogs didn't judge my qualifications.

Not one frog looked at me and said: Wait, aren't you also exhausted? Shouldn't you fix yourself before you try to help me?

They just accepted the help. From imperfect hands attached to an imperfect person who was also struggling. Because help is help, even when it comes from someone who's also drowning. Even when the hands that rescue you are trembling.

Help doesn't require perfection. It requires willingness. It requires noticing. It requires the small amount of strength you have left after you think you have none.

I have a friend named David. He's an alcoholic — sober now for eight years, but still an alcoholic. Still attends meetings twice a week. Still calls his sponsor when the urge gets loud. Still struggles some days.

He sponsors three other alcoholics. Shows up at 2 a.m. when they call in crisis. Talks them through cravings. Offers support when they're on the edge of relapsing.

He does this while still being an alcoholic himself. While still needing support from his own sponsor. There's no finish line where you're done being an alcoholic and now you're qualified to help. There's just: recovery while helping others recover. Struggling while helping others through their struggles.

He's drowning — slowly, carefully, with support — and still throwing ropes to people who are drowning faster. He's the frog and the frog-mover. Both. Always.

And it works. Maybe because there's no distance. No hierarchy. No I'm better than you, let me help you get to my level. Just: I'm also struggling. I have this one thing I've learned. Let me share it with you while we both struggle together.

Helping while struggling creates something pure helping can't.

When you help from a place of having-it-all-together, there's a gap. An implicit hierarchy: I have what you need. Let me pull you up to my level.

That kind of helping can work. But there's something more powerful when you help from a place of also-struggling. No distance. No gap.

Just: I see you on the sidewalk. I'm also on a sidewalk. Let me move you anyway. Even though I also need moving. Even though my hands are shaking.

The person being helped doesn't feel judged. Doesn't feel like they're being rescued by someone looking down at them with pity. They feel seen by someone who understands. Moved by hands that also tremble. And somehow, that lands deeper. That feels more real.

You can be the frog and the frog-mover at the same time.

You're allowed to need help while helping others. Allowed to be a mess while cleaning up other people's messes. Allowed to be drowning while throwing ropes.

This isn't noble self-sacrifice. This isn't giving from an empty cup. This is recognizing: you're never just the frog or just the frog-mover. You're always both. Everyone is always both.

The person helping you is also struggling. The person you're helping might turn around and help you tomorrow. The roles aren't fixed. The categories aren't permanent.

We're all frogs on sidewalks. We're all trying to help each other off our respective sidewalks. We're all drowning and throwing ropes simultaneously.

That's not a failure of self-care. That's just how it actually works when humans help humans instead of maintaining artificial hierarchies about who's qualified to help whom.

Two years after that first frog night, my marriage ended. I don't talk about this much — it's complicated and involves another person's story that isn't mine to tell. But the relevant part: I was falling apart. Completely. Couldn't sleep. Lost fifteen pounds because I kept forgetting to eat. Spent entire days just trying to function and entire nights lying awake wondering how I'd failed so completely.

I was a frog on the biggest sidewalk of my life.

During that same period, my friend Jennifer was going through her own crisis. Her father was dying — slowly, painfully — and she was trying to be present for him while working full-time and parenting two young kids. She called me one night, crying. Completely overwhelmed.

I should have said: I can't help you right now. I'm barely surviving my own crisis.

I didn't say that. I listened. For an hour. Let her cry. Let her talk through what she was feeling. Offered what support I could from my own empty place. Not because I was strong enough. But because she needed help and I could give it even though I also needed it desperately.

And after that call, I felt less like I was drowning. Not because her problems made mine seem smaller. Not because I was distracting myself. But because throwing that rope — reaching outside my own drowning to help someone else — reminded me: I'm not completely useless. I can still make a difference even when I'm falling apart.

That reminder helped me survive that night. And the next night. And the month after that.

I helped her. She helped me by letting me help her. Both of us were drowning. Both of us survived.

This is how we actually make it through.

Not by waiting until we're strong to help others. Not by fixing ourselves first. But by noticing: someone is struggling. I'm also struggling.

Let me help anyway. Especially because I'm also drowning.

Because helping them helps me. Because being needed reminds me I still matter. Because the both/and is the truth about how humans actually survive. The both/and is what keeps us all afloat when we're all drowning together.

You don't have to not-be-a-frog to move frogs.

You can be stuck and still move other stuck things. Vulnerable and still help other vulnerable things. Small and struggling and barely making it, and still stop to help someone else who's small and struggling and barely making it.

Not because you're strong. But because you see. And you care. And you have just enough — barely enough, but enough — to help.

Ten frogs moved while I was a frog myself. Three years later, I'm still both. Still the frog. Still the frog-mover.

That's not a contradiction. That's just the truth about being human.

So if you're reading this from your own sidewalk, from your own stuck place:

Look around. Who else is stuck? Who else needs help?

And help them. Even though you're also stuck. Even though you also need help.

Not because you're qualified. Not because you're stable or strong or together enough. But because they need it. And you can give it. Even in your brokenness. Especially in your brokenness.

Because your brokenness qualifies you. Your struggle gives you vision. Your drowning helps you see other people drowning.

You can be a frog and still move frogs. Both. Always. Without contradiction.

That's how we all make it across the sidewalk. Together. All of us stuck, all of us moving each other, all of us making it somehow.

Not because we're strong. Because we're willing to help even when we also need help.

That's enough. That's always been enough. That's how we survive.

FROG STEPS: CHAPTER 12 TAKEAWAYS

The Small Truth: You don't have to be fixed to help fix things. Your brokenness doesn't disqualify you — it qualifies you. You can be drowning and still throw ropes. Being the frog and the frog-mover at the same time isn't contradiction — it's reality.

The Frog Wisdom: The frogs didn't check my credentials before accepting help. They accepted it from imperfect hands attached to an imperfect person who was also struggling. Because help is help, even when it comes from someone who's also stuck.

The Practice: Look for someone who's struggling while you're struggling. Offer help even though you also need help. Notice what happens: Do you feel less alone? Does throwing a rope while drowning actually help you stay afloat too?

The Question: Who could you help today, even though you're also struggling? What if your own stuckness makes you better qualified to help, not less? What if drowning and throwing ropes at the same time is exactly how we all survive?

CHAPTER 13: MOVING FROGS IS A PRACTICE, NOT AN ACHIEVEMENT

I kept walking after that first September night.

Not every evening. Not with discipline or consistency or any particular plan. Just: sometimes. When I needed to move. When the day had been too much. When sitting still felt dangerous.

And I kept finding frogs. Not every walk. Not even most walks. But often enough that moving frogs became part of the walk. Part of how I move through the world now.

Some nights I'd move three. Some nights none. Some nights — after particularly heavy rains — I'd move fifteen, twenty, losing count somewhere around twelve because I was just moving them on autopilot. Kneeling and carrying and setting down, over and over.

It became something I did. Not something I decided to do. Just something that happened when I walked and there were frogs.

I'll never "complete" moving frogs.

There's no finish line. No achievement unlocked. No certificate of completion where I'm officially a Master Frog Mover and can retire from the practice.

Frogs will always end up on sidewalks after rain. As long as it rains. As long as frogs exist. As long as I walk. And that's not a failure of the system. That's just what it is. Things get stuck, rain happens, help is needed, again and again, forever.

We treat everything like a project with an endpoint.

Lose weight. Build habits. Transform your life. Achieve your goals. All of it framed as: Do this thing until it's done. Complete the transformation and then you're transformed. Cross the finish line and then you're finished.

But nothing that matters actually works that way. There's no endpoint to being healthy — you just keep making choices that support health. No completion to being a good parent — you just keep showing up. No finish line to being a writer — you just keep writing.

The things that matter most are the things you never finish. The things you just keep doing. The things that become part of who you are rather than things you check off a list.

Practice, not project. Process, not destination.

Moving frogs is practice.

Some walks I'm paying attention — scanning the sidewalk, looking for small brown shapes in the streetlight. Some walks I'm lost in my own head and I probably miss frogs I would have seen if I'd been present.

Some seasons I walk three or four times a week. Some seasons I barely walk at all. Winter comes. Work gets busy. Depression hits and I can't make myself leave the house. Weeks pass, maybe months, without a single walk, without a single frog moved.

None of that makes me good or bad at moving frogs. It just makes me someone who practices moving frogs. Imperfectly. Inconsistently. Ongoing.

The practice doesn't judge me for the walks I miss. It just continues when I return. Always there. Always available.

Practice doesn't require perfection.

I've stepped over frogs without seeing them. Walked past when I was too tired to stop. Chosen convenience over helping and kept walking even knowing that was probably wrong.

And all of that is okay. Because practice isn't about perfection. Practice is about returning. Again and again. Imperfectly. Inconsistently. But returning.

The practice doesn't demand perfection. It just invites participation. Whenever you're ready.

Whenever you show up again after weeks or months of not showing up.

The practice is still there. Still yours.

The practice shapes you over time.

Before that night three years ago, I wouldn't have stopped for a frog. Would have walked right past. Too busy, too distracted, too consumed by my own problems to notice small vulnerable things.

Now I stop. Not every time — still imperfect, still miss some. But I stop. I notice. I help when I can.

The practice changed me. Slowly. Through repetition. Through choosing to stop and help, again and again, imperfectly and inconsistently, but again and again over three years.

I'm not a better person now than I was three years ago — that's not what this is about. I'm just a person who practices stopping. Who practices noticing small vulnerable things. Who practices believing that small actions matter.

The practice shaped me into someone who does that. Not perfectly. Not every time. But regularly enough that it's part of who I am now. Part of how I move through the world.

Practice creates identity through repetition.

You don't become a writer by writing perfectly. You become a writer by writing. Again and again. Badly and well. Inconsistently but repeatedly.

The repetition creates the identity. Not the perfection. Not the achievement. Just the doing, repeated over time, until "person who writes" becomes part of who you are rather than something you're trying to become.

I'm a person who moves frogs. Not because I move every frog or never miss a walk. But because I move frogs — repeatedly, over three years, imperfectly but repeatedly. If you asked Anna to describe me, "moves frogs on walks" would probably make the list. That identity was built through nothing more than imperfect repetition.

The practice doesn't end.

There will always be frogs on sidewalks. There will always be rain that brings them out. There will always be small vulnerable things that need help.

This isn't a problem to solve. It's just reality. I can't fix it. Can't prevent it. All I can do is keep walking. Keep noticing. Keep stopping. Keep helping. One frog at a time. Imperfectly. For as long as I'm able.

Not achieving mastery. Not completing a transformation. Just: keep walking, keep noticing, keep helping. Some days better than others. Some seasons more than others. Some years barely at all because life gets hard and the practice gets forgotten.

But the practice continues. Because the frogs continue. Because the rain continues. Because I continue to have the capacity — small, imperfect capacity — to help when I notice.

Practice is humble.

It doesn't claim mastery. Doesn't pretend to have arrived. Doesn't demand recognition.

I'm not a frog-moving expert. I'm just a person who practices moving frogs. Who sometimes does it well and sometimes doesn't. Who sometimes shows up and sometimes fails to.

And that's enough. The imperfect ongoing returning is enough. That's what makes it sustainable — not the perfection, not the achievement, just the willingness to keep practicing. Even when you're bad at it. Even when you miss weeks or months. Even when you fail more than you succeed.

The practice doesn't care. It just continues. And welcomes you back every time you return.

Practice is sustainable.

Projects burn you out. Achievements create pressure. Transformations demand constant upward trajectory.

But practice just asks you to return. To try again. To keep going. No pressure to be perfect. No judgment when you fall off. No shame for the gaps.

Just: come back. Try again. Imperfectly. That's enough.

I can sustain this. Can keep walking, keep noticing, keep helping for another ten years. Another thirty if I'm lucky. Not because I'm disciplined or consistent. Because the practice doesn't demand those things. It just asks me to show up when I can. To help when I notice. To practice when I'm able.

That's sustainable. Because it accepts my humanity. Works with my reality instead of demanding I become someone I'm not.

Practice allows for seasons.

Some seasons I walk every day. The weather's perfect, my energy's good, frogs are everywhere. Some seasons I barely go outside: winter too cold, depression making leaving the house impossible, work consuming every available hour.

Some seasons I'm highly attuned to frogs, scanning every sidewalk. Some seasons I'm so consumed by my own struggles that I miss most of them.

All of that is part of practice. The practice adapts to seasons. Allows for rhythms. Accepts reality.

Unlike achievements — which demand constant forward progress regardless of circumstances — practice allows for ebb and flow. For good seasons and hard seasons. The practice is still there through all of it. Still available. Still waiting for you to return whenever you're ready.

Three years in, I'm still learning. Still missing frogs I should have seen. Still walking past when I should stop. Still imperfect. Still inconsistent. Still human.

And that's the practice. Not mastery. Just ongoing imperfect returning to the thing that matters.

Moving frogs when I can. Walking when I can. Helping when I can. Noticing when I can.

Not perfectly. Not always. But repeatedly. For three years. And for however many years remain.

That's enough. The practice is enough.

The frogs keep appearing. The rain keeps falling. The practice keeps continuing.

And I keep showing up. Imperfectly. But showing up.

That's all practice asks. That's all any of us can do.

FROG STEPS: CHAPTER 13 TAKEAWAYS

The Small Truth: Moving frogs isn't a project with an endpoint — it's a practice. Practice doesn't require perfection, just returning. The practice shapes you through repetition, creates identity through consistency, and continues forever because the need for help continues forever.

The Frog Wisdom: There's no frog-moving achievement to unlock. No point where you've moved enough frogs and you're done. Just: frogs keep appearing, rain keeps falling, sidewalks keep existing. The practice continues. Imperfectly. Forever. And that's not a problem — that's just what practice is.

The Practice: Choose one small thing you want to practice — not achieve, not complete, but practice. Then practice it. Imperfectly. Miss days. Come back. Miss more days. Come back again. Let the practice shape you through repetition without requiring perfection.

The Question: What would change if you treated more of your life as practice instead of project?

What if there's no endpoint, just ongoing imperfect returning to the things that matter?

CHAPTER 14: SOMETIMES THE FROG YOU SAVE IS YOU

I moved a frog last Tuesday.

Small one. Maybe the size of a nickel. Right in the middle of the sidewalk under a streetlight, exactly like that first frog three years ago. Same spot, almost. Same streetlight. Same wet concrete. Same Missouri evening after rain.

I knelt down. Scooped it up — cold, wet, trembling in my palm. Carried it fifteen feet to grass. Set it down gently. Watched it freeze for maybe ten seconds before it hopped once, twice, then disappeared into darkness.

The same action I've done hundreds of times now. The same small movement. The same tiny help that shouldn't matter but somehow does.

But this time, something was different.

This time, I saw both of us clearly — the frog I was moving and the frog I used to be. And the person I've become through three years of stopping and helping and noticing and moving.

This time, I understood completely: I was the frog I was moving. All along. Every single time.

Every time you help someone else, you're also helping yourself.

Not metaphorically. Not in some abstract philosophical way where karma balances or what goes around comes around. But actually. Concretely. Immediately.

Because the help you give shapes who you become. The frog you move changes the person who moves it. The practice of noticing and helping creates a version of yourself that notices and helps.

You save the frog. The practice saves you. Not eventually. Not as a side effect. Right now. In the act. Through the doing.

Three years ago I was drowning.

Stuck in the wrong job. Wrong city. Wrong life. Exhausted beyond exhaustion. Becoming smaller and quieter and less like myself with each passing week.

I was the frog on the sidewalk. Frozen. Vulnerable. Exposed. Needing help desperately.

And then I went for a walk. And I moved frogs. And in moving them, I practiced something I desperately needed to practice: noticing small vulnerable things and doing something about them.

I practiced seeing stuckness. Responding to vulnerability. Helping even when I was also drowning. Believing that small actions matter. Moving forward three inches at a time.

That practice saved me. Not because moving frogs solved my problems — the job was still wrong, the city still didn't fit. But moving frogs changed who I was. Turned me into someone who stops. Who helps. Who notices. Who has something to give even when feeling empty.

That version of me could leave the wrong job. Could move back to Missouri. Could write this book. Could cross his own sidewalk.

The frog-moving practice created the person capable of moving himself.

You become what you practice.

Practice judgment, you become judgmental. Practice cynicism, you become cynical. Practice helplessness, you become helpless.

Practice helping, you become helpful. Practice noticing, you become observant. Practice moving small things, you become someone who can move.

The frogs I moved taught me how to move myself. Not through magical transfer of wisdom. Not because there was some grand cosmic plan. Just through repetition. Through doing the thing — stopping, noticing, helping, moving — again and again until that thing became part of who I am.

Three hundred frogs moved over three years created a person who knows how to move. Who believes movement is possible. Who trusts that small actions compound. Who can cross sidewalks three inches at a time even when the destination isn't visible.

Helping others helps you see your own situation more clearly.

When I was stuck in that wrong job, I couldn't see it clearly. Couldn't name what was wrong. Couldn't trust my own knowing. Just felt vaguely miserable and told myself I should be grateful. Told myself I was being dramatic.

But when I saw frogs on sidewalks, I saw instantly: Wrong place. Doesn't belong here. Needs to be moved.

No ambiguity. No second-guessing. No "maybe it's fine, maybe I'm overreacting."

Just: This frog is in the wrong place. That needs to change. Right now.

And in seeing that about the frogs with such clarity, I started seeing it about myself.

The frogs gave me language for my own stuckness. Gave me permission to acknowledge it. If the frog doesn't deserve to stay on the sidewalk just because it ended up there, neither do I. If the frog's stuckness is reason enough to help it, my stuckness is reason enough to help myself.

The frogs taught me that I was worthy of rescue. Not because I'd earned it. But because being stuck is enough. Needing help is enough.

Helping others gives you permission to help yourself.

There's something about helping a frog that makes it impossible to maintain the story that you're too broken to be helped. That your situation is too complicated. That you don't deserve rescue because you got yourself into this mess.

Because if a frog deserves help just for being stuck — no questions about how it got there, no requirement that it prove itself worthy — then so do you.

If I can see a frog and immediately know this needs help without hesitation or qualification, then I can extend that same knowing to myself. Can trust my own assessment of wrongness. Can believe my own need for help is valid.

Worthiness isn't something you earn. It's something you have by virtue of being stuck. By virtue of being in a wrong place. That's always been enough.

Sometimes you have to save something else before you can save yourself.

I couldn't see how to save myself three years ago. Couldn't figure out the first step. Couldn't imagine the path from where I was to where I needed to be.

But I could see how to save a frog. That was clear. That was possible. That was three inches of movement I could actually make.

So I did that. Again and again. And in doing that — in practicing saving small things I could save — I learned how to save myself.

Not through dramatic revelation. But through the accumulated practice of noticing stuckness and responding to it. Through three years of small movements that taught me: Small movements matter. Movement is possible. You don't need to see the whole path to take the next step.

All the lessons. All the truths. All the wisdom I needed to cross my own sidewalk — I learned it from frogs. From moving them. From practicing on them before I practiced on myself.

I saved frogs. The practice saved me.

The help goes both ways.

The frogs didn't know they were teaching me. Didn't know that every time I moved them, I was practicing moving myself. They were just trying to survive. Just hopping toward grass. Just doing what frogs do.

And I was just trying to help. Just responding to something small and vulnerable that needed help.

But we helped each other. I moved them to safety. They taught me how to move to safety. Both of us survived September and all the Septembers that came after.

The help went both ways. It always does. Because helping isn't a one-way transaction where the strong help the weak and nothing flows back. Helping is a circle. A loop. A mutual exchange where everyone involved gets something they need.

We saved each other. Frogs and frog-mover. Practicing together. Surviving together.

Last Tuesday, when I moved that small frog, I saw both of us clearly:

The frog that was stuck — exposed on concrete, vulnerable to everything bigger and faster, frozen by fear and confusion, needing help to reach grass that was only feet away.

And the frog I used to be — exposed in a wrong job, vulnerable to systems bigger than me, frozen by fear and exhaustion, needing help to reach the life I knew existed somewhere.

And the person I've become through three years of stopping and helping and noticing and moving — someone who knows how to see stuckness, take three-inch hops, trust that small movements matter, help even when drowning, practice even when imperfect.

I saved that frog. And in saving hundreds of frogs over three years, I saved myself.

Not perfectly. Not completely. Not in some dramatic transformation where everything's fixed.

But truly. Really. Enough.

I'm off my sidewalk now. Not because I leaped. Not because someone dramatically rescued me. But because I practiced moving small things three inches at a time. And that practice taught me how to move myself three inches at a time. And three inches became three hundred. And three hundred became across the sidewalk. And across the sidewalk became a different life entirely.

The frog I saved was me. All along. Every single time.

If you're reading this from your own sidewalk right now — stuck and scared and can't see how to save yourself — I want you to know:

Start by saving something else.

Find a frog. Find something small that needs help. And help it. Not because you're avoiding your own problems. But because helping will teach you how to help yourself. Because moving other stuck things will show you how to move yourself.

The frog you save might actually be you. The practice that helps them might be the practice that saves you. The three inches they hop might teach you how to hop your own three inches.

Save them. Let the practice accumulate. Let the lessons compound. Let the movement you create for them teach you how to create movement for yourself.

Three years from now, you'll look back and realize: You moved. You crossed the sidewalk. You made it to grass.

Not because you leaped. Not because you had perfect clarity. But because you practiced. On frogs. On small things. On whatever needed help while you also needed help.

The practice saved you. Just like it saved me.

The frog you save is you. Always. Every time.

FROG STEPS: CHAPTER 14 TAKEAWAYS

The Small Truth: Every time you help someone else, you're practicing helping yourself. The frog you move teaches you how to move. The help goes both ways — you save them, the practice saves you. You become what you practice, and practicing helping creates someone capable of being helped.

The Frog Wisdom: The frogs didn't know they were teaching me how to save myself. They were just trying to survive. But in helping them survive, I learned how to survive. The practice accumulated until I had enough to move myself.

The Practice: Help something small this week. A frog. A person. A project. Notice what you learn about helping while you're helping. Notice what the practice teaches you about your own stuckness. Let helping others show you how to help yourself.

The Question: What if the best way to save yourself is through practicing saving others? What if the frog you move today is actually you, learning how to move?

CHAPTER 15: KEEP WALKING

It's been three years since that first September night.

Three years of walking. Three years of noticing. Three years of stopping and moving and helping when I can.

I haven't moved a frog in two weeks. Haven't walked much at all. It's been a busy month. A hard month. A month where I barely had enough energy for myself, let alone for noticing small vulnerable things that needed help.

And that's okay. That's the practice. That's what sustainability looks like.

The practice doesn't require daily perfection.

Some weeks I walk every night. The weather's perfect, my energy's good, frogs are abundant. I move dozens.

Some weeks I don't walk at all. Winter comes and it's dark by five. Work explodes. Depression hits and leaving the house feels impossible. Life happens and walking is the first thing to go.

Some months I move dozens of frogs. Some months I move none. Don't walk. Don't help. Don't practice at all. Just survive. Just get through.

Just do the absolute minimum required to keep existing.

All of that is okay. All of that is the practice. It doesn't require consistency — just willingness to return. Whenever you can. Whenever you're ready.

Three years later, I'm still learning.

Still figuring out when to stop and when to keep going. Still making mistakes. Still missing frogs I should have seen. Still walking past when I should stop.

The practice doesn't make you perfect. It just makes you someone who practices. Someone who tries, fails, learns, and tries again. Someone who shows up imperfectly but shows up.

That's enough. That's all the practice asks.

Three years later, there are still frogs on sidewalks.

The problem didn't get solved. The need didn't disappear. More rain came. More frogs emerged. More creatures ended up in wrong places.

And that's okay. Because the practice isn't about eliminating need — it's about responding to need when you encounter it. About helping when you can. About doing something. Small something. Three-inch something. But something.

That has to be enough. Because that's all any of us can do. Notice what we can notice. Help what we can help. Move what we can move. Three inches at a time. Imperfectly. For as long as we're able.

Three years later, I'm still the frog sometimes.

Still end up on sidewalks. Still get stuck. Still freeze when I should hop.

Last month I got paralyzed on a project. Frozen by fear it wouldn't be good enough. Couldn't move forward for two weeks. Still the frog. Still vulnerable. Still capable of ending up in wrong places even after three years of learning how to cross sidewalks.

The practice didn't cure me. Didn't make me immune to stuckness. It just gave me tools. The ability to recognize: I'm stuck. This is a sidewalk. I need to move — or I need to freeze before I hop — or I need to hop three inches even though three inches doesn't feel like enough.

I'm still the frog. And I'm still the person who moves frogs. Both. Always. That hasn't changed. Won't ever change. But now I know that both roles are okay. Both are necessary. Both are part of being human in a world where rain falls and frogs emerge and help is always needed and always available if you're willing to ask or willing to give.

Three years later, the small movements have added up.

Three hundred words became twenty thousand became thirty-five thousand became this book you're holding right now.

One frog became ten frogs became hundreds of frogs became a practice, an identity, a way of being in the world.

Three inches became three feet became across the sidewalk became a different life entirely.

None of the individual movements felt significant. Most of them felt too small to matter. But they accumulated. Compounded. Added up to transformation that happened so slowly I didn't notice until I looked back and saw: I'm not where I was. I'm not who I was.

From wrong job to right work. From wrong city to right place. From drowning to breathing. From stuck to moving.

Three inches at a time. For three years. Until three inches became everything.

Three years later, I know: the practice works.

Not perfectly. Not quickly. Not dramatically. But truly.

Small movements compound. Three-inch hops cross sidewalks. Helping others helps you. Freezing and hopping both count. Progress isn't linear. You don't need to see the destination. Rain creates movement. Practice creates identity.

All of it true. All of it proven through three years of walking and noticing and helping and moving. Not through theory — through practice.

The practice works. Even when it doesn't feel like it's working. Even when you can't see how three inches today will matter three months from now.

I'm proof. The frogs are proof. This book is proof.

So here's what I want to tell you at the end:

Keep walking.

Even when you're tired. Even when the sidewalks are empty and there are no frogs to move and the practice feels pointless. Keep walking.

Keep noticing. Keep stopping when you can. Keep moving small things three inches at a time. Keep practicing even when you're bad at it.

With breaks and gaps and seasons where you barely practice at all. With mistakes and failures and walks where you miss every frog because you're too lost in your own head. Keep practicing.

Because the movements compound. The three inches matter. The frogs survive. You survive. We all survive together through nothing more than small repeated imperfect actions that don't feel like enough but somehow always are.

And when you can't — when you're too tired or too stuck or too much of a frog yourself — that's okay too. The practice will wait. The frogs will keep appearing. The opportunity to help will return when you're ready.

It's Tuesday evening as I write this. Late October in Missouri. It rained earlier today. The streets are wet.

There are probably frogs on sidewalks right now.

I'm going to walk. Not because I've mastered anything. Not because I always notice or always stop or always help. But because the practice continues. Because I still have working legs and working hands and a working heart that still cares about small vulnerable things.

I'll move what I can. Notice what I notice. Take my three-inch hops through whatever the evening brings.

That's the only ending I can offer you. Not "and then everything was perfect." Not "and I never struggled again." Just: I keep walking. The practice continues. The frogs keep getting moved. The three inches keep adding up.

And somehow, that's enough. It's always been enough. It always will be enough.

So walk. Tonight if you can. Tomorrow if you can't. Whenever you're ready.

Notice the frogs on your particular sidewalks. Move the ones you can. Help when you have capacity. Practice when you have the will.

Three years from now — or ten, or thirty — you'll look back and realize: You moved. You crossed the sidewalk. You made it to grass.

Not because you leaped. Not because you were strong or certain or fearless or consistent. But because you walked. You noticed. You stopped. You helped. You hopped.

Three inches at a time. Imperfectly. For however long it took.

Until imperfect became enough. Until three inches became transformation. Until the frog you saved was yourself.

Keep walking. The rest will follow.

The frogs taught me that. And they've never been wrong.

There is no takeaway for Chapter 15. The walking is the takeaway.

THE END

Keep hopping.

EPILOGUE: YOUR FIRST WALK

I found the frog on a Tuesday. Nothing special about that Tuesday. I wasn't looking for metaphors or life lessons. I was just walking, same route I'd walked a hundred times before, when I saw something small and stuck. And here's the thing about small and stuck: once you start seeing it, you can't stop. You'll notice the shopping cart someone left in the middle of the parking space. The toy car wedged under the couch. The email you've been meaning to send for three weeks. The drawer that won't close because something's jammed in the track.

Small things. Stuck things.

And every single one of them is whispering the same question: What are you going to do about it?

THE CHALLENGE

This isn't about transforming your life in seven days. This isn't about becoming someone new or fixing everything that's broken or finally getting your shit together. This is about walking.

Noticing. Moving one small thing. That's it.

Here's how it works:

DAY 1: JUST WALK

Go outside. Walk for ten minutes. Don't listen to a podcast. Don't plan your day. Don't solve problems. Just walk. Notice what you notice. The crack in the sidewalk. The house with the overgrown hedge. The way the light hits the trees.

You're not looking for anything. You're just looking.

Write down one thing you saw. Anything. It doesn't have to mean something.

DAY 2: FIND SOMETHING STUCK

Walk the same route. This time, look for something that's stuck.

Could be anything:

- A plastic bag caught in a fence

- A rock blocking a storm drain
- A sign that's fallen over
- Something out of place

Don't fix it yet. Just notice it.

Write it down: "I saw ____________ and it was stuck because ____________."

DAY 3: IDENTIFY YOUR THREE-INCH HOP

Now think about your own life.

What's one small thing that's stuck? Not the big stuff, not your career or your marriage or your entire future.

Something small:

- A drawer that won't close
- A text you haven't sent
- A book you started and abandoned
- A plant that needs repotting

Pick ONE thing. Write it down.

Then ask yourself: What's one three-inch hop I could take?

Not the whole solution. Just the first tiny move.

DAY 4: TAKE THE HOP

Do it.

Move the thing. Send the text. Clear the drawer. Repot the plant.

It doesn't have to be perfect. It doesn't have to solve everything.

Just do the three-inch thing.

Then write down how it felt. Not what you accomplished, how it felt to move something that was stuck.

DAY 5: NOTICE THE FREEZE

Walk again.

This time, when you see something stuck, pay attention to what happens in your body before you decide whether to help. Do you tense up? Look away? Start making excuses? That's the freeze. That's the moment we all have, the split second where we decide whether something is "our problem" or not.

You don't have to fix anything today. Just notice the freeze.

Write it down: "When I saw ____________, I felt ____________."

DAY 6: HELP SOMETHING SMALL

Today, when you're out walking, move one stuck thing. Pick up the branch blocking the path. Straighten the fallen sign. Move the shopping cart back to the corral. Something small. Something that takes less than a minute. No one has to see you do it. You don't get credit. You don't get thanks. You just... help. Then keep walking.

Notice how that feels too.

DAY 7: REFLECT

Last walk.

Same route. Same ten minutes. But this time, ask yourself:

What did I learn about being stuck?

What did I learn about moving?

What do I want to keep doing?

Write it down. All of it. The messy thoughts, the half-formed ideas, the things you're not sure about yet.

You don't have to have answers. You just have to keep walking.

WHAT HAPPENS NEXT?

Maybe nothing. Maybe you finish this challenge and go back to your regular life and forget all about frogs and three-inch hops.

That's okay.

Or maybe—just maybe—you start noticing the stuck things everywhere. And maybe you start moving them. Not because you have to. Not because someone's watching. But because you can. Because you're someone who walks. Someone who notices. Someone who helps small things.

And that's not nothing. That's how change happens. That's how the world gets a little bit better. One frog at a time. One hop at a time. One walk at a time. So. What are you waiting for?

Go take a walk.

ACKNOWLEDGMENTS

To the readers who will walk after reading this. Who will notice frogs. Who will take three-inch hops. Who will keep going when keeping going is hard. Thank you for practicing. Thank you for walking. Thank you for believing that small movements matter.

And to the frogs. Literally. The small brown creatures on Missouri sidewalks who didn't know they were teaching me but taught me anyway. You showed me that vulnerability isn't weakness.

That small doesn't mean worthless. That three inches is enough. That freezing and hopping both count. That help goes both ways. That the frog you save might be yourself.

ABOUT THE AUTHOR

Dan Jayce is a veteran of the U.S. Air Force where he served honorably as a Security Policeman for four years. After his time in the service, Dan built a thirty-year career in education, counseling, and workforce development. He taught at Meijo University in Japan in addition to delivering one-to-one training and professional seminars for professors, doctors, engineers, business executives, and government officials, including on-site at Toyota Corporation and Mitsubishi Heavy Industry. As a Certified Workforce Development Professional, he spends his days helping people, organizations, and communities navigate real, lasting change. These books weren't written from theory. They were written the same way he teaches, by doing the work first, then showing others the path.

If you'd like to share your own frog stories, he'd love to hear them. Because we're all in this together, crossing sidewalks three inches at a time, helping each other when we can, being helped when we need it.

www.bamboorootspublishing.com
instagram.com/ danjayce

Frogs Helping Frogs

This book wouldn't be complete without naming some of the human frogs that I have had the honor of calling friends.

Scott W., Roddy R., Amy W. Randall H., Rosie V., Stephen B., Jeff V., K.K., M.J., Kirk Q. Roberta W., Tina L., just to name a few.

I have seen you move frogs. Thank you.

www.ingramcontent.com/pod-product-compliance
Lightning Source LLC
LaVergne TN
LVHW090517110826
845146LV00003B/897